The Joy

The Happy Habit

You have been an amazing by therapist and social worker!

Reverend Drew

I appreciate all your great help!

Drew W

Introduction

Part 1

The Happy Habit

Part 2

The Joy-filled Christian

ISBN-13: 978-1535335621
ISBN-10: 1535335629
Copyright 2016
Reverend Drew

www.faithhopelove.us

Introduction

"May the God of hope fill you with all joy and peace in believing, that you may abound in hope by the power of the Holy Spirit (Romans 15:4)."

Jesus wants us to have joy. Jesus tells us in John 15:11, "These things I have spoken to you, that My joy may remain in you, and *that* your joy may be full."

Jesus reveals the greatest commandment in Mark 12:30-31, "And you shall love the Lord your God with all your heart, with all your soul, with all your mind, and with all your strength.' This *is* the first commandment. And the second, like *it, is* this: 'You shall love your neighbor as yourself.' There is no other commandment greater than these (also stated in Matthew 22:37 and Luke 10:27)." I wanted to begin this short work with the words of Jesus. When we love as Jesus commands us, inner joy is the result. We can have joy, true inner joy, if we love.

Joy and love go together as we see in Galatians 5:22-23, "But the fruit of the Spirit is love, joy, peace, longsuffering, kindness, goodness, faithfulness, gentleness, self-control. Against such there is no law." Joy is the next fruit of the Spirit after love. Love and joy are connected because as we learn to accept Jesus' love and His finished work on the cross, our inner joy increases. Joy is about looking up, not around at our circumstances.

Joy is composed of many aspects to include gratitude. Joy and gratitude are also connected as we see in 1 Thessalonians 5:16-18, "Rejoice always, pray without ceasing, in everything give thanks; for this is the will of God in Christ Jesus for you."

The word we know as "joy" comes from the Greek word "Chairo." This Greek word means to rejoice, be glad, to rejoice exceedingly, to be well, thrive, to be cheerful, calmly happy, favorably disposed and leaning towards. The Greek *chara* is closely related to *chairo*, which means "grace" or "a gift." *Chara* is the normal response to *chairo*—we have joy because of God's grace.

We after we are saved through confession of Jesus Christ as Lord and believe in our heart that God raised Him from the dead (Romans 10:9), the next step is to allow the Holy Spirit to increase our joy from the natural to the supernatural through a deep and abiding relationship with Christ Jesus.

Our inner joy is then expressed through outward actions. You will see after reading this book how the joy of Jesus Christ will become your strength and foundation. I can testify that sometimes joy can be so great it is inexpressible (1 Peter 1:8). Most importantly, it means "to delight in God's grace" or literally to experience God's grace (favor) or be conscious for His grace. The New Testament mentions 'Chairo' 68 times.

Joy should be normal state of the born-again believer because of the work and promises of God through His Son Jesus. Joy is an expression of faith which pleases God. We should be joyful because of God's kingdom—His influence on earth (Romans 14:17). The Spirit's production of joy can manifest in several different ways:

The joy of deliverance: When God sets someone free, rejoicing is in order.

1 Samuel 2:1: Hannah was filled with joy at her deliverance from her enemies.

Acts 12:14: The servant girl was so overjoyed that God had rescued Peter from prison that she forgot to let Peter in the house.

The joy of salvation: Our greatest reason to be joyful is that God wants to save us and spend eternity with us. Nothing is better than this.

Luke 15:7: All heaven is joyful when a person accepts God's provision of salvation.

Acts 8:8: The people of Samaria were joyful as they heard the gospel and saw God's power in healing the sick.

Acts 13:52; 15:3: Jewish believers rejoiced when they heard of the work of the Holy Spirit in saving Gentiles.

The joy of spiritual maturity: As the Holy Spirit works in us to bear more fruit, we become confident in God's promises and rejoice in our walk with Him and with other believers.

John 15:11: The fullness of joy comes to those who continue in the love of Christ and obey Him.

2 Corinthians 1:24; 2:3; 7:4; 1 Thessalonians 2:19-20; 3:9: Paul knew joy as the churches gave evidence of the Holy Spirit working among them.

Philippians 2:2: Groups of believers who unite in demonstrating the mind, love, and purpose of Christ bring joy to others.

Hebrews 10:34; 12:2; James 1:2-4: Believers, following the example of Jesus, endure persecution because of the promise of future joy.

The joy of God's presence: The Holy Spirit draws us to God, in whose presence we can know true joy. Without the Holy Spirit, no one would seek God.

Psalm 16:11: "You will fill me with joy in your presence, with eternal pleasures at your right hand."

Matthew 2:10; Luke 1:14: Mary and the shepherds were joyful because Immanuel had been born.

Matthew 28:8; Luke 24:41: The women who went to Jesus' tomb and the disciples were overjoyed that He rose from the dead.

Joy is a gift from God and receiving His joy is a choice. We choose whether to value God's presence, promises, and work in our lives. When we yield to the Spirit, He opens our eyes to God's grace around us and fills us with joy (Romans 15:13). Joy is not to be found in a fallen world; it is only fellowship with God that can make our joy complete (1 John 1:4).

This work will focus on the Joy of the Lord and how any believer can make joy a daily habit. Joy is a type of "calm happiness" as defined earlier. Joy and happiness is possible through Christ Jesus. I call it the "happy habit", choosing joy through purposeful living and walking in the Spirit.

This book is broken into two sections; the happy habit and the joy-filled Christian. I hope this book encourages, empowers and delivers you from anything hindering you or keeping you from living the abundant life that Jesus spoke of in John 10:10 when he said, "I have come that they may have life, and that they may have *it* more abundantly."

"Faith is a living, bold trust in God's grace, so certain of God's favor that it would risk death a thousand times trusting in it. Such confidence and knowledge of God's grace makes you happy, joyful and bold in your relationship to God and all creatures. The Holy Spirit makes this happen through faith. Because of it, you freely, willingly and joyfully do good to everyone, serve everyone, suffer all kinds of things, love and praise the God who has shown you such grace. Thus, it is just as impossible to separate faith and works as it is to separate heat and light from fire!" Martin Luther

God bless you!

Part 1

Habits

A **habit** is a routine of behavior that is repeated regularly and tends to occur subconsciously.

In the <u>American Journal of Psychology</u> (1903) it is defined in this way: "A habit, from the standpoint of psychology, is a more or less fixed way of thinking, willing, or feeling acquired through previous repetition of a mental experience." Habitual behavior often goes unnoticed in persons exhibiting it, because a person does not need to engage in self-analysis when undertaking routine tasks. Habits are sometimes compulsory. The process by which new behaviors become automatic is **habit formation**. Old habits are hard to break and new habits are hard to form because the behavioral patterns we repeat are imprinted in our neural pathways, but it is possible to form new habits through repetition.

As behaviors are repeated in a consistent context, there is an incremental increase in the link between the context and the action. This increases the automaticity of the behavior in that context. Features of an automatic behavior are all or some of: efficiency, lack of awareness, unintentionality, and uncontrollability.

Habit formation is the process by which a behavior, through regular repetition, becomes automatic or habitual. This process of habit formation can be slow. It has been researched that habits can occur in as little as 18 days but can take as long as 254 days.

As the habit is forming, it can be analyzed in three parts: the cue, the behavior, and the reward. The cue is the thing that causes the habit to come about, the trigger of the habitual behavior. This could be anything that one's mind associates with that habit and one will automatically let a habit come to the surface. The behavior is the actual habit that one exhibits, and the reward, a positive feeling, therefore continues the "habit loop". A habit may initially be triggered by a goal, but over time that goal becomes less necessary and the habit becomes more automatic.

Some habits are known as "keystone habits", and these influence the formation of other habits. For example, identifying as the type of person who takes care of their body and is in the habit of exercising regularly, can also influence eating better and using credit cards less. In business, safety can be a keystone habit that influences other habits that result in greater productivity (source of the above is Wikipedia).

Will and intention

A key factor in distinguishing a bad habit from an addiction or mental disease is willpower. If a person has control over the behavior, then it is a habit. Good intentions can override the negative effect of bad habits, but their effect seems to be independent and additive—the bad habits remain, but are subdued rather than cancelled.

--

Eliminating bad habits

Many techniques exist for removing established bad habits, e.g., *withdrawal of reinforcers*—identifying and removing factors that trigger and reinforce the habit. The basal ganglia appears to remember the context that triggers a habit, so habits can be revived if triggers reappear. Recognizing and eliminating bad habits as soon as possible is advised. Habit elimination becomes more difficult with age because repetitions reinforce habits cumulatively over the lifespan. According to Charles Duhigg, there is a loop that includes a cue, routine and reward for every habit. An example of a habit loop is TV program ends (cue), go to the fridge (routine), eat a snack (reward). The key to changing habits is to identify your cue and modify your routine and reward.

Bad habits must be changed with determination and God's help. I John 3:9 TLB states, "The person who has been born into God's family does not make a practice of sinning, because now God's life is in him; so he can't keep on sinning, for this new life has been born into him and controls him—he has been born again."

Bad habits deserve no mercy. Deuteronomy 12:2-3, TLB states, "You must destroy all the heathen altars wherever you find them—high in the mountains, up in the hills, or under the trees. Break the altars, smash the obelisks, burn the shameful images, cut down the metal idols, and leave nothing even to remind you of them!"

Fill your life with good habits. Titus 2:7 NKJV states, "In all things showing yourself to be a pattern of good works; in doctrine showing integrity, reverence, incorruptibility."

Form the habit of focusing your thoughts on good things. Philippians 4:8 TLB states, "Fix your thoughts on what is true and good and right. Think about things that are pure and lovely, and dwell on the fine, good things in others. Think about all you can praise God for and be glad about."

What good habits can we start and maintain? Tithing is an excellent habit to develop. Deuteronomy 14:22 TLB states, "You must tithe all of your crops every year."

Jesus modeled a habit of worship we should imitate. Luke 4:16 NIV states, "He went to Nazareth, where He had been brought up, and on the Sabbath day He went into the synagogue, as was his custom. And He stood up to read."

Prayer is a valuable habit. Matthew 6:5 NIV states, "And when you pray, do not be like the hypocrites, for they love to pray standing in the synagogues and on the street corners to be seen by men. I tell you the truth, they have received their reward in full."

In Charles Duhigg's book the Power of Habit, Why we do what we do and how to change, he explains that "habits emerge because the brain is constantly looking for ways to save effort." Duhigg explains the habit loop, "the process with our brain is a three-step loop. First, there is a cue, a trigger that tells your brain to go into automatic mode and which habit to use. Then there is the routine, which can be physical or mental or emotional. Finally, there is a reward, which helps your brain figure out if this particular loop is worth remembering for the future. Over time, this loop becomes more and more automatic. The cue and reward become intertwined until a powerful sense of anticipation and craving emerges. Eventually, a habit is born. When a habit emerges, the brain stops fully participating in decision making. It stops working so hard, or diverts focus to other tasks. So unless you deliberately fight a habit – unless you find new routines – the pattern will unfold automatically."

This is how habits work in the natural but as believers, we have Jesus and the Holy Spirit to help us transform our thinking and renew our minds. When we accepted Christ, we no longer do it on our own power. We are new creatures and have the Holy Spirit working within us. Habits never really disappear according to some doctors. They are encoded into the structures of our brain but through Christ we are new creatures and can be transformed by the renewing of our minds.

Duhigg explains that we can "learn to create new neurological routines that overpower those behaviors – if we take control of the habit loop – we can force those bad tendencies into the background. Habits, as much as memory and reason, are at the root of how we behave. We might not remember the experiences that create our habits, but once they are lodged within our brains the influence how we act –often without our realization.

This is why it's so important to constantly examine ourselves. 2 Corinthians 13:5 states, "Examine yourselves to see whether you are in the faith; test yourselves. Do you not realize that Christ Jesus is in you--unless, of course, you fail the test?" I will mention this verse again because it's very important for every believer to keep this verse in the forefront of our mind.

Duhigg further explains, "you can never truly extinguish bad habits. Rather, to change a habit, you must keep the old cue, and deliver the old reward, but insert a new routine. That's the rule; if you use the same cue, and provide the same reward, you can shift the routine and change the habit. Almost any behavior can be transformed if the cue and reward stay the same. If you want to change a habit, you must find an alternative route, and your odds for success go up dramatically when you commit to changing as part of a group. Belief is essential, and it grows out of a communal experience, even if that community is only as large as two people."

For the believer in Christ Jesus, all things are possible even the most difficult bad habits.

"But Jesus looked at *them* and said to them, "With men this is impossible, but with God all things are possible."

I wanted to explain how habits work in the natural, but we have a supernatural God who can do the impossible (Matthew 19:26)."

Jesus changes the game for all those who confess Him as their Lord and Savior.

Below are some bible verses which will help you change your old habits.

"Do not be conformed to this world, but be transformed by the renewal of your mind, that by testing you may discern what is the will of God, what is good and acceptable and perfect (Romans 12:2)."

No temptation has overtaken you that is not common to man. God is faithful, and he will not let you be tempted beyond your ability, but with the temptation he will also provide the way of escape, that you may be able to endure it (1 Corinthians 10:13)."

"All things are lawful for me," but not all things are helpful. "All things are lawful for me," but I will not be enslaved by anything (1 Corinthians 6:12)."

"And he said, "What comes out of a person is what defiles him. For from within, out of the heart of man, come evil thoughts, sexual immorality, theft, murder, adultery, coveting, wickedness, deceit, sensuality, envy, slander, pride, foolishness. All these evil things come from within, and they defile a person (Mark 7:20-23)."

"My son, be attentive to my words; incline your ear to my sayings. Let them not escape from your sight; keep them within your heart. For they are life to those who find them, and healing to all their flesh. Keep your heart with all vigilance, for from it flow the springs of life. Put away from you crooked speech, and put devious talk far from you (Proverbs 4:20-27)."

"Therefore be imitators of God, as beloved children (Ephesians 5:1)."

"Not neglecting to meet together, as is the habit of some, but encouraging one another, and all the more as you see the Day drawing near (Hebrews 10:25)."

"Let the thief no longer steal, but rather let him labor, doing honest work with his own hands, so that he may have something to share with anyone in need (Ephesians 4:28)."

"Be imitators of me, as I am of Christ (1 Corinthians 11:1)."

"A wise son hears his father's instruction, but a scoffer does not listen to rebuke. From the fruit of his mouth a man eats what is good, but the desire of the treacherous is for violence. Whoever guards his mouth preserves his life; he who opens wide his lips comes to ruin. The soul of the sluggard craves and gets nothing, while the soul of the diligent is richly supplied. The righteous hates falsehood, but the wicked brings shame and disgrace (Proverbs 13:1-25)."

"Pray without ceasing (1 Thessalonians 5:17)."

"What then? Are we to sin because we are not under law but under grace? By no means! Do you not know that if you present yourselves to anyone as obedient slaves, you are slaves of the one whom you obey, either of sin, which leads to death, or of obedience, which leads to righteousness? (Romans 6:15-16)."

"To the choirmaster. A Psalm of David. How long, O Lord? Will you forget me forever? How long will you hide your face from me? How long must I take counsel in my soul and have sorrow in my heart all the day? How long shall my enemy be exalted over me? Consider and answer me, O Lord my God; light up my eyes, lest I sleep the sleep of death, lest my enemy say, "I have prevailed over him," lest my foes rejoice because I am shaken. But I have trusted in your steadfast love; my heart shall rejoice in your salvation (Psalm 13:1-6)."

"Do not lie to one another, seeing that you have put off the old self with its practices and have put on the new self, which is being renewed in knowledge after the image of its creator (Colossians 3:9-10)."

"My son, do not forget my teaching, but let your heart keep my commandments, (Proverbs 3:1)."

"Of David, when he changed his behavior before Abimelech, so that he drove him out, and he went away. I will bless the Lord at all times; his praise shall continually be in my mouth (Psalm 34:1)."

What does the Bible say about habits?

The Bible does not specifically speak of "habits" as such. However, much is said about the meaning of the word: "a thing done often, and hence, usually done easily; an act that is acquired and has become automatic." We all have habits, whether good or bad. Even newborns may come into this world with the habit of already sucking their thumbs. However, for the Christian, the whole of their lives is one of being transformed by the renewing of our minds (Romans 12:2). This implies exchanging old (bad) habits for new (good) ones, in order to please the Lord. For instance, "Do all things without grumbling and complaining" (Philippians 2:14) may demand a new habit on our part. We may need to cultivate a whole new pattern of thinking, from negative to positive as "we take captive every thought to make it obedient to Christ." (2 Corinthians 10:5).

God's command "Do not steal" means that we must cultivate the habit of being honest in all things. This may require a whole new habit for some. It is the "putting off" of our old nature and "putting on" of the new nature we are given when we are born spiritually into God's family (Colossians 3:9-10). This is not an easy thing to do and is, in fact, impossible in our own strength. But Paul reminds us, "I can do all things through Christ, who strengthens me" (Philippians 4:13).

Regarding habits pertaining to health issues, such as taking drugs, smoking, drinking, sexual immorality, etc., we are told, "Do you not know that your body is a temple of the Holy Spirit, who is in you, whom you have received from God? You are not your own. You were bought at a price. Therefore honor God with your body" (1 Corinthians 6:19-20). "Do not get drunk on wine, which leads to debauchery. Instead, be filled with the Spirit" (Ephesians 5:18).

For those who belong to Jesus Christ, forming new habits by being controlled by the Holy Spirit becomes a way of life. These new habits are described by Jesus as loving Him. Jesus replied, "If anyone loves me, he will obey my teaching. My Father will love him, and we will come to him and make our home with him"

(John 14:23). Most importantly, we are told, "And whatever you do, do all to the glory of God."

There are some habits that the believer must cultivate each day:

1) Praise/worship (opposite of pride)

2) Holiness/Purity of heart (living righteous) (opposite of lust)

3) Repentance (opposite wrath)

4) Obedience (& sacrifice) (opposite of gluttony and having no self-control)

5) Service (selflessness) working for God (opposite of greed)

6) Humility/humble (opposite of envy)

7) Gratitude (opposite of sloth/laziness)

The 7 deadly sins are

pride, greed, lust, envy, gluttony, wrath and sloth.

What are the habits of a joy-filled happy Christian? Jesus said that He came to Earth that we might have an abundant life full of joy and triumph. Practice these joy habits and start living your life to the fullest:

1. Joy-filled habit of focusing on the joy of the Lord.

   Blessed (happy, fortunate, prosperous, and enviable) is the person who walks and lives not in the counsel of the ungodly, nor stands in the path where sinners walk, nor sits down where the scornful gather - Psalm 1:1

   Do your actions match what you say you believe? Is the Word of God being animated in the way you behave, speak and treat others? There is abundant joy in the presence of the Lord. Go there daily in prayer, worship and reading the Bible and make sure your everyday life is aligned and disciplined by Kingdom power.

2. Joy-filled habit of making God the center of your life.

   Unless the Lord builds the house, those who build it labor in vain. Unless the Lord watches over the city, the watchman stays awake in vain - Psalm 127:1

3. We need to make sure we're following the Lord's agenda and program and not trying to build apart from Him. This verse reminds us to build our lives separate from God and to focus solely on self will be of no use to us in the end. Entrust your life to God and bring about a life full of joy and eternal value.

4. Joy-filled habit of integrity.

   The integrity of the upright guides them - Proverbs 10:9

   It's not enough to have sound moral principles and Christian beliefs. We need to be living this out so that our beliefs are producing fruit in our life. Honesty, sincerity and uprightness should be continually lived out in our daily life. Integrity serves as a guide to create boundaries for joyful living.

5. Joy habit mentoring and council

A wise man will hear, and will increase learning; and a man of understanding shall attain unto wise counsels - Proverbs 1:5

Discipleship is about mentoring and being mentored in the body of Christ. We should have trusted individuals that are allowed to speak and have influence through providing godly wisdom. We should also be that for someone else. Life is an interpersonal journey designed for you to be a blessing to others while being blessed yourself.

6. Joy-filled habit of being slow to anger.

My dear brothers and sisters, take note of this: Everyone should be quick to listen, slow to speak and slow to become angry - James 1:19

Nothing will steal your joy faster than being easily annoyed, frustrated or angry. It's interesting that the Bible doesn't tell us to never be angry. We're given specific guidelines to master our anger: *don't let the sun go down on your anger, good sense makes one slow to anger and anger lodges in the fool's bosom.* The next time you get angry ask yourself is it worth more than protecting your joy and peace.

7. Joy-filled habit of honoring others.

Honor everyone - 1 Peter 2:17

Practice honoring others by respecting and seeing the value in those around you. God has placed gifts, talents and His ability in each and every person we meet. Recognize that and encourage it to come forward every chance you get.

- -

8. Joy-filled habit of admitting when you are wrong.

   But he gives us more grace. God opposes the proud-but gives grace to the humble - James 4:6

   Jesus says His strength is made perfect in our weakness, so when we're wrong or make mistakes -- to respond in humility -- is to say "God I need you to help me here." This is why the humble receive more and more grace. Being proud is dangerous because it drives us to be self-reliant to the point where we forget our life Source.

9. Joy-filled habit of service and love

   For you were called to freedom, brethren. Only do not use your freedom as an opportunity for the flesh, but through love serve one another - Galatians 5:13

10. Love to serve and serve to love. As much as you can bring the Kingdom of God into your circle of influence through sharing your God-given gifts, talents and abilities. Fruitful living in this way will have a ripple effect for years to come.

Five Habits that will sabotage your joy

1. Comparing

   Living your life always looking out will prevent you from seeing what God is doing in your life. Looking at what others have is a recipe for disaster. Because no matter what, someone will always be smarter, better-looking, richer, more successful or better-liked than you. Living your life always looking out will prevent you from seeing what God is doing in your life.

2. Complaining

   No matter what is going on in their lives, happy people don't complain. They have a realistic awareness of hardships, but they never fixate on those things. They can be honest when they are struggling, but they don't allow their mouths to utter words of negativity about the world around them, because they know that what comes out of their mouths is always a reflection of what is going on inside their hearts. Your mouth is a powerful instrument, so be sure to use it to speak good things. When the enemy tempts you to dwell on all that you don't have, defeat him by praising God for all that He's given.

3. Competing

Happy people don't live their life with others as their measuring stick. They don't compete in an effort to get ahead or be the best, because their value is not rooted in how others are doing, but rather on what God says. Those who are in constant competition with others find themselves on an emotional roller-coaster, sometimes getting ahead, sometimes falling behind. Happy people root their value in Christ. And that is a value unchanging.

4. Controlling

I love the serenity pray which reads, "Lord, grant me the peace to accept the things I cannot change, the courage to change the things I can, and the wisdom to know the difference." Happy people understand that some things in life cannot be controlled, and they learn to let go of those things. But here's the thing about letting go: It only becomes a reality when we grasp the truth that the moment we let go, God is in control.

5. Criticizing

People who put others down the most are the ones who are struggling the most within themselves. It's true that the people who put others down the most are the ones who are struggling the most within themselves. Happy people can easily find the good in others and can just as easily find it in themselves.

It's never too late to start transforming the way we think, the things we speak and the way we interact with the world around us. "Happiness" as the world defines it may not always be possible, but no matter where you are in life, you have the ability to choose joy.

Many people spend their lives waiting to be happy. You may think, "if only I had more money," or "could lose weight," or you fill in the blank, then I would be happy. Well here's a secret: you can be happy right now. It's not always easy, but you can choose to be happy, and in the vast majority of circumstances there's no one who can stop you except for yourself.

The truth is, happiness doesn't come from wealth, perfect looks or even a perfect relationship. Happiness comes from within. This is why, if you truly want to be happy, you need to work on yourself, first.

Dr. Mercola wrote the following article entitled "22 Positive Habits of Happy People" which I believe can help anyone.

1. Let Go Of Grudges

Forgiving and forgetting is necessary for your own happiness, as holding a grudge means you're also holding onto resentment, anger, hurt and other negative emotions that are standing in the way of your own happiness. Letting go of a grudge frees you from negativity and allows more space for positive emotions to fill in.

2. Treat Everyone With Kindness

Kindness is not only contagious, it's also proven to make you happier. When you're kind to others, your brain produces feel-good hormones and neurotransmitters like serotonin and you're able to build strong relationships with others, fostering positive feelings all around.

3. Regard Your Problems As Challenges

Change your internal dialogue so that anytime you have a "problem" you view it as a challenge or a new opportunity to change your life for the better. Eliminate the word "problem" from your mind entirely.

4. Express Gratitude For What You Have

People who are thankful for what they have are better able to cope with stress, have more positive emotions, and are better able to reach their goals. The best way to harness the positive power of gratitude is to keep a gratitude journal or list, where you actively write down exactly what you're grateful for each day. Doing so has been linked to happier moods, greater optimism and even better physical health.

5. Dream Big

Go ahead and dream big, as you'll be more likely to accomplish your goals. Rather than limiting yourself, when you dream big you're opening your mind to a more optimistic, positive state where you have the power to achieve virtually anything you desire.

6. Don't Sweat The Small Stuff

If the issue you're mad about will be irrelevant a year, a month, a week or even a day from now, why sweat it? Happy people know how to let life's daily irritations roll off their back.

7. Speak Well of Others

It may be tempting to gather around the office water cooler to get and give the daily gossip, but talking negatively about others is like taking a bath in negative emotions; your body soaks them up. Instead, make it a point to only say positive, nice words about other people, and you'll help foster more positive thinking in your own life as well.

8. Avoid Making Excuses

It's easy to blame others for your life's failures, but doing so means you're unlikely to rise past them. Happy people take responsibility for their mistakes and missteps, then use the failure as an opportunity to change for the better.

9. Live in The Present

Allow yourself to be immersed in whatever it is you're doing right now, and take time to really be in the present moment. Avoid replaying past negative events in your head or worrying about the future; just savor what's going on in your life now.

10. Wake Up At The Same Time Every Morning

Getting up at the same time every day (preferably an early time) is deceptively simple. Doing so will help regulate your circadian rhythm so you'll have an easier time waking and likely feel more energized. Plus, the habit of rising early every day is one shared by many successful people, as it enhances your productivity and focus.

11. Don't Compare Yourself To Others

Your life is unique, so don't measure your own worth by comparing yourself to those around you. Even regarding yourself as better than your peers is detrimental to your happiness, as you're fostering judgmental feelings and an unhealthy sense of superiority. Measure your own success based on your progress alone, not that of others.

12. Surround Yourself With Positive People

The saying "misery loves company" is entirely true. That's why you need to choose friends who are optimistic and happy themselves, as you will be surrounded with positive energy.

13. Realize That You Don't Need Others' Approval

It's important to follow your own dreams and desires without letting naysayers stand in your way. It's fine to seek others' opinions, but happy people stay true to their own hearts and don't get bogged down with the need for outside approval.

14. Take Time To Listen

Listening helps you soak in the wisdom of others and allows you to quiet your own mind at the same time. Intense listening can help you feel content while helping you gain different perspectives.

15. Nurture Social Relationships

Positive social relationships are a key to happiness, so be sure you make time to visit with friends, family and your significant other.

16. Meditate

Meditation on scripture because it helps you keep your mind focused, calms your nerves and supports inner peace. Research shows it can even lead to physical changes in your brain that make you happier.

17. Eat Well

What you eat directly impacts your mood and energy levels in both the short and long term. Whereas eating right can prime your body and brain to be in a focused, happy state, eating processed junk foods will leave you sluggish and prone to chronic disease.

18. Exercise

Exercise boosts levels of health-promoting brain chemicals like serotonin, dopamine, and norepinephrine, which may help buffer some of the effects of stress and also relieve some symptoms of depression. Rather than viewing exercise as a medical tool to lose weight, prevent disease, and live longer – all benefits that occur in the future – try viewing exercise as a daily tool to immediately enhance your frame of mind, reduce stress and feel happier.

19. Live Minimally

Clutter has a way of sucking the energy right out of you and replacing it with feelings of chaos. Clutter is an often-unrecognized source of stress that prompts feelings of anxiety, frustration, distraction and even guilt, so give your home and office a clutter makeover, purging it of the excess papers, files, knick knacks and other "stuff" that not only takes up space in your physical environment, but also in your mind.

20. Be Honest

Every time you lie, your stress levels are likely to increase and your self-esteem will crumble just a little bit more. Plus, if others find out you're a liar it will damage your personal and professional relationships. Telling the truth, on the other hand, boosts your mental health and allows others to build trust in you.

21. Establish Personal Control

Avoid letting other people dictate the way you live. Instead, establish personal control in your life that allows you to fulfill your own goals and dreams, as well as a great sense of personal self-worth.

22. Accept What Cannot Be Changed

Everything in your life is not going to be perfect, and that's perfectly all right. Happy people learn to accept injustices and setbacks in their life that they cannot change, and instead put their energy on changing what they can control for the better.

I wanted to add a few other suggestions for the joy-filled Christians.

Wake up feeling grateful

As they wake up, they always feel grateful for being alive, for the gift of life and for the joy of a new day. When things are bad, make a list in your mind of all the positives. Research shows clearly that people who regularly express gratitude are less likely to suffer from loneliness, anxiety, depression or envy.

Never skimp on breakfast

They know that this is the <u>most important meal</u> of the day. It provides you with all the essential nutrients, minerals and energy you are going to need for the day. Planning a good breakfast the night before is also a good idea. You will be able to get some of the things ready so you can save time when you are under pressure during your morning schedule.

They plan their good deeds

It should come as no surprise to learn that when happy people help others it increases their happiness, rather than being a burden. Studies published in the *Journal of Happiness Studies* illustrate this clearly. Other studies show that these happier and kinder people will live much longer.

They rarely ruminate about the past

Happy people have one thing in common. They very rarely express regrets about the past. They know that life is for living now and that to-day is the main event. They never let it be hijacked by the past or yesterday's failures.

They make happiness a habit

Did you know that as much as 40% of your daily activities is sheer habit or routine? You are on auto-pilot half the time. Happy people make gratitude, joy and mindfulness a part of that habit and it always works for them, especially in the morning.

They reject the morning distractions

Happy people know that they do not want those distractions form news, emails and text messages muscling in too early. They will damage their early morning serenity in getting their gratitude and mindfulness act together. This is what is important. Those messages can wait till much later. This also helps them to approach all the deadlines, meetings and tasks with much more serenity.

They have set their daily goals

Happy people know what when they do start work, they should try and get the most difficult task done first. It is just part of a list of objectives but they have always clear goals and have prioritized what they want to get done. It increases their happiness. Richard Davidson, a neuroscientist at the University of Wisconsin has researched all this. He found that when you see progress towards achieving a difficult task or goal, this increases happiness and also suppresses all the negative emotion.

The Book of Proverbs 6:16-19, among the verses traditionally associated with King Solomon, it states that the Lord specifically regards "six things the Lord hateth, and seven that are an abomination unto Him", namely:

"A proud look

A lying tongue

Hands that shed innocent blood

A heart that devises wicked plots

Feet that are swift to run into mischief

A deceitful witness that uttereth lies

Him that soweth discord among brethren."

Another list, given this time by the Epistle to the Galatians (Galatians 5:19-21), includes more of the traditional seven sins, although the list is substantially longer: adultery, fornication, uncleanness, lasciviousness, idolatry, sorcery, hatred, variance, emulations, wrath, strife, seditions, heresies, envyings, murders, drunkenness, revellings, "and such like". Since the apostle Paul goes on to say that the persons who practice these sins "shall not inherit the Kingdom of God", they are usually listed as (possible) mortal sins rather than capital vices.

How can we become highly effective Christians? In other words, how do we emulate Christ more in secular settings and be "on mission" as believers to share our love of Jesus with others? Let's look at the Bible and see whether we have any examples with whom to emulate. Daniel lived in a foreign land and kept his practices. Job trusted God despite his loss of everything. Paul was faithful unto his death. I propose that rather than trying to obey commands or practice learned doctrines, they developed certain habits which sustained them. Paul wrote about these habits in chapter twelve of Romans and chapter five of Ephesians: do not be proud but maintain a contrite heart, be joyful patient and faithful, keep up spiritual fervor, share with those in need, love sincerely, hate evil but cling to good, and live in harmony with other believers. These habits can make living in the world but not of the world as natural as breathing.

Christianity cannot exist without a humble heart.

FIRST HABIT

The first habit is to not be proud but maintain a contrite heart, have genuine sorrow for the wrong we've done. When I write about pride I'm talking about the pride of life, the lust of the flesh, and the lust of the eyes. Adam and Eve suffered from this type of pride and it caused them to disobey God. Adam and Eve sought their own will instead of God's will. They believed the devil when he said, "You won't really die." Today, many well intentioned people are guilty of the same sin. We have been tricked into believing what God calls evil is a matter of freedom of choice, in the same way Adam and Eve were tricked. We believe the devil when he says, "It's not really a sin." The first habit we need to practice is to get rid of our pride and obey God. The second part of that habit is to maintain a humble heart. Christianity cannot exist without a humble heart.

When we have done something to cause unintentional harm to someone we tend to feel terrible about it and wish we could undo the behavior. We feel badly in our hearts for hurting someone. That feeling is what I call a contrite heart. For example the wise men told Herod about the birth of a king. Herod had all male babies less than two years of age in Bethlehem killed. Had the wise men heard about the murders they would have had contrite hearts. When we realize that our sin put Jesus on the cross and he died in our place, he went to the cross where we should have gone (Rom 5:8); it becomes easy to feel contrite. With a contrite heart we become willing never to cause more harm and will live for Jesus because the only way to appease the feeling is to do right to the one we've hurt.

SECOND HABIT

Another habit is to be faithful in prayer. The past year has seen unusual and catastrophic events of nature. I found it interesting to watch people being interviewed who suffered such events. Some of the people were thanking God to be alive and trusting him to provide for them. Other people were cursing the government because handouts were not coming fast enough. Eventually the damage will be repaired. Christians know that good and bad things happen to everyone. Highly effective Christians remain joyful, patient, and faithful despite their circumstances. Our witness to others and our testimony will be revealed by how we respond. What Christian wants God to hear him or her cursing the government because nature destroyed our homes?

THIRD HABIT

Paul wrote that we should never lack in zeal but keep our eagerness while serving the Lord. Last year a local pastor was shot in the head by some youth who were trying to forcefully enter a teen center he supervised. He survived the shooting, returned to the youth center, and resumed his duties. A near fatal gunshot wound would be enough to cause many people to quit, but this pastor maintained his strong desire to serve God. Today, his message to the youth is that if he cared enough for them to risk his life, they should care enough for themselves to risk their own lives in trying to change.

We should walk in love by being imitators of God.

In chapter seven of the book of Acts, Stephen was persecuted but never lost his zeal even up to his death. Stephan actually asked God to not hold their sin against them before he died.

FOURTH HABIT

We are daily tempted to place value on things that don't matter. What matters is how we can make a difference in the lives of other people. Share with those in need, practice hospitality until they become our next habit. Opportunities to share can come unexpectedly. Sometimes we are so busy we do not recognize them. Instead of viewing them as an inconvenience, we need to take advantage of those opportunities when they happen.

Many of us would like to show brotherly love. Little acts of caring, doing what is right just because it is what Jesus would do, can show love in a big way. Jesus said to love your neighbor as yourself.

FIFTH HABIT

The next habit should be easy but for some reason it takes a long time to develop. Love must be sincere, be devoted to each other in brotherly love. You may have heard about the Greek words for different types of love. Eros, romantic love; storge, family love; agape, Godly love; philos, love of everything else, sometimes called friendship love (philosophy is love of wisdom, philharmonic is love of harmony, audiophiles love music). Love "always protects, always trusts, always hopes, always perseveres" (1 Corinthians 13: 7).

SIXTH HABIT

Do not repay evil for evil. Hate what is evil, cling to what is good. This habit is explained in Ephesians chapter five as walking in wisdom. Realizing we are filled with the Spirit we can avoid behaviors such as drunkenness, filthy language and coarse joking. Christians simply cannot drink excessively with their non-Christian friends, and engage in coarse conversation with them. We will never be a good witness of Christ in that way. Instead they may mock us behind our backs and be repelled from Christ. We have a mission to make disciples, and sitting in a bar or other environment getting drunk and telling coarse stories will not accomplish that mission.

SEVENTH HABIT

The last habit for effective Christians is live in harmony with each other. When we are fully developed spiritually we can see beyond ourselves and consider how what we do may affect other people. The Bible says we can tell who Christians are by our love. We need to walk in unity. Unity does not mean we all agree on everything but it does mean we walk in lowliness toward each other, considering the worth of the other person. We need to be longsuffering, or patient. If we have to forgive someone seventy-times seven on the same day, what is wrong with that? Jesus would do the same for us. We need to have a gentle spirit toward other people. Jesus is a great example. He is God but always put others first. Everything will seem strange as long as we live in a sinful world. Our own flesh is one of our enemies but we can overcome the flesh by developing habitual behaviors.

We need to let Jesus teach us to see him more clearly, know him more intimately, long after him more deeply, and praise him more sincerely. We cannot let anything deter us from our quest to come closer to the heart of God

Habits of self-mastery

"Mastery of self should be our ultimate goal because it aligns our purpose with God's plans for our lives and is demonstration of the ninth fruit of the Spirit."

The ninth fruit of the spirit is self-control and it comes from the Greek word "Egkrateia" which is defined as self-control or self-mastery (the virtue of one who masters his desires and passions, esp. his sensual appetites). This concept is given to the believer as part of the new creature in Christ. We already have self-control imparted in us through our faith in Christ. We just have to receive this free gift from God.

Proverbs 23:7 is one of my life verse. "For as a man thinketh in his heart, so is he." This verse allowed me to reconfigure my life along the spiritual lines which are pleasing to God. In the Gospel of Mark, Jesus repeats something similar when he says, "There is nothing that enters a man from outside which can defile him; but the things which come out of him, those are the things that defile a man (Mark 7:15). This is expounded on in verses 20-23 when Jesus says, "What comes out of a man, that defiles a man. For within, out of the heart of men, proceed evil thoughts, adulteries, fornications, murders, thefts, covetousness, wickedness, deceit, lewdness, an evil eye, blasphemy, pride, foolishness. All the evil things come from within and defile a man." This is why it's so important to live that new life which is possible once we start to do things differently. Do something different today that is truly good for you.

For example, do something radically different which you've previously have been reluctant to do: such as attending a Bible study, going to a different church service -- for example, attend the early or late service, reading the Bible today for an hour, go to a soup kitchen and volunteer, volunteer at your church today -- ask the minister what you can do even if its sweeping the floor, pray for that person you have a grudge against, praying that God blesses their life, call that friend or family member you have a resentment against, tell them you love them - nothing else, be the light in the world that you want to see. This should be in addition to anything you are already doing, not in place of. The purpose of this exercise is to do something for someone else with honest intention, without the expectation of anything in return.

Our loving and merciful God "desires that everyone be saved and to come to the knowledge of truth" (1 Timothy 2:4). An anonymous author wrote the following short poem: *"A careless word may kindle strife, A cruel word may wreck a life; a timely word may lessen stress, a loving word may heal and bless."*

Proverbs 13:3 states, "He who guards his mouth preserves his life." We have the power to speak blessings over our life or death. It's your choice.

The adversary (Satan) is always there waiting to bring us down. Satan uses people in our lives, sometimes Satan uses people who love us. Now these people are living a life of illusions just as we were before we decided to gain mastery of self. Once we gain mastery of ourselves and are able to escape the illusions, we can then help others come to the truth. We have to be gentle with others living in darkness so that we can bring others to the light. Thus do not be upset at those still living in the darkness, those who do not know how to master themselves.

Those living in darkness are still our best teachers. From those in the darkness, we are able to be reminded of what we do not want to be. Those who are not loving, or those who get angry quickly or the prideful or the unforgiving need to be shown the way. We can be that light in the world. We need to understand what the devil is trying to do. The devil and his agents hate us. The devil wants to bring us down. The devil is targeting us each and every day. The devil is in a battle for our hearts and minds. The devil suits up each day in order to insert his programming into our heads. When we do not respond, the devil adjusts to make us uncomfortable or to take us away from our game plan. The devil hates humanity. The devil wants all of us to fall like he fell.

The devil started a plan against humanity many years ago. The devil exists and hangs his hopes on people believing that he does not exist. I believe that some people do his bidding every day just as the demons did years before. The devil wants to win our hearts and mind. The devil does not want you to master yourself. The devil wants you to be out of control in every way. The devil wants you to be petty, vengeful, unforgiving, ego-driven, envious, jealous, angry, hateful, and selfish as well as feeling any other negative feeling. The devil does not want you to look inside. The devil loves drift and procrastination. The devil inspires us to make excuses and to do anything else except read God's word.

God has a plan for your life as stated in Jeremiah 29:11. "For I know the thoughts that I think toward you, says the LORD, thoughts of peace and not of evil, to give you a future and a hope.

The devil also has a plan for your life. The devil wants you to be disagreeable and to lead a defeated life. The devil's battle plan would go something like this:

The Devil's Battle for Humanity's Eternal Soul

Goal: To lead all humans to the pits of hell. To win the hearts and minds of the humans.

Weapons available to the devil: Reality TV, tabloids, internet porn, depression, anything promoting idols (perhaps even a show U.S. or some other nation state with the name Idol in it), drugs/alcohol, hate, prejudice and narrow-mindedness.

Tools available to promote disbelief: Sin to include judging others, pride (a great tool), fear, selfishness, unforgiveness, anger, hatred, etc.

Budget: Unlimited resources

Difficulty in recruiting people to work against the humans: No difficulty

Opposition: God gave the humans free will so we will not have to worry about him. (Note, we will do another campaign to make people believe that there is no God. We will seek to keep people away from the churches or reading the bible. Look for opportunities to promote drugs and alcohol to aid in the permanent fall of man as this allows man to keep his hearts and minds away from God. Make people believe that they have no choice but to suffer.)

Potential Problems: Need to eliminate prayer, love, and hope in the world.

Devil's Motto: Life sucks or Blame God for all of your problems. Or to make you believe that there is no God.

We can succumb to the devil's plan or not. With God, anything is possible because He gave us a choice. When I wrote this section, I started to get mad thinking about how the devil was trying to win my heart and mind. I think that we all need to get mad at what the devil is trying to do to us. The devil, the enemy, the adversary, the evil one, Satan are all names for that force operating in the world pushing us to not live up to our potential. If depression is a tool used by the devil then passion is a tool that God loves. God wants us to be passionate for Him and to love Him with all of our hearts, minds, soul, and strength. Do not give your hearts and minds to the devil. I know I gave mine to the devil for too many years. I took a step towards God.

James 4:8 states, "Draw near to God, and he will draw near to you" This is a promise. If we do our part, God promises to do His part.

The devil is trying to influence you without your knowledge, you can choose not to be a part of it anymore. Self-awareness will free you.

"Be still and know that I am God," from Psalm 46:10 lets us know that we need to slow down at times. The devil loves when we run around unfocused or focused on too many things. If we are unsteady in our mind then it's easy for the devil to win. We need to still our minds. We need to listen to what God is trying to say in our lives. God speaks to us through circumstances, people, biblical scriptures, sermons, and through spending quiet time with Him.

The devil does not want you or me to master our mind. The devil sends distractions into our lives in order to take our focus off God.

The devil loves when we blame God for crisis or tragedy. The devil does not like when we are excited about life and have hope.

Anthony Robbins in *Awaken the Giant Within* states, "*Too many of us leave ourselves at the mercy of outside events over which we may have no control, failing to take charge of our emotions -- over which we have all the control -- instead relying on short-term quick fixes (p.26).*" The devil loves short-term fixes. I like how Anthony Robbins talks about mastering oneself. He says that three decisions we all make every moment of our lives which control our destiny. "*1) Our decision about what we focus on; 2) Our decision about what things mean to us; and 3) Our decisions about what to do to create the results we desire (p.40).*"

I have made up a short cheat sheet for ABC's of Mastery of Self:

Assess your fearlessly to determine where you need work!

Believe in yourself because you are God's workmanship!

Choose life, happiness so you can have a better life!

Develop the qualities that make you better. Don't limit yourself!

Execute the necessary steps to achieve your goals!

Fix your stuff, fix your faults. If you don't deal with your stuff, then you force others to deal with it. Fight the right battles.

Good is the goal: You must think good thoughts, speak good words, and do good things all the time!

Hope Boldly each day!

Invest in yourself-time, energy, and effort as well as others!

Jump up for joy! Get excited about life!

Kindness: Show kindness to yourself and others!

Love Big! Laugh often!

Master yourself: body, mind, and spirit!

Never surrender to sadness or depression!

Open-minded to new ideas and beliefs. Open to change!

Pray boldly each day! Passion leads to power!

Questions: Ask the right questions in order to change!

Recruit happiness by choosing your attitude each day and changing your habits!

Spot the issues of concern in your life and the conditioning of your past!

Take charge of your life!

Unleash the fire inside of you!

Victory is in Jesus Christ! A God consciousness leads to victory!

Winner: You are a winner through Christ because our Lord won the victory!

X an unknown quantity in math -- X is the amount of love (unlimited) that can fit in your heart and that you can give to God and others.

Y Yearn for meaning and purpose in your life.

Zest for life! Live with a zest in your life!

I decided to make sure to provide a summary so that people could master themselves so the devil's covert influence program would not be successful. If we look at the environment in which we live, the tricks of the devil become clearer. Use an infallible source, God's word in the Bible, to master yourself. The Bible contains details on the enemy and how to successful navigate the world we live in. The truth is readily available for those who seek it.

In John 15: 15-16, Jesus says, "You did not choose Me but I chose you and appointed you that you should go and bear fruit, and that your fruit should remain, that whatever you ask the Father in my name He may give you. These things I command you, that you love one another." We have access to great power through love. Jesus tell us to love many time because we (me included) are a stubborn bipedal species, we are hardheaded and want to do it our way. But our ways are not His ways and our ways will lead us to defeat and brokenness.

I love the following verse: "Delight yourself also in the Lord and He shall give you the desires of your heart" (Psalm 37:4). How do we delight in the Lord? By loving Him with all of our hearts and loving others. We cannot expect to receive God's great gifts when we disobey Him. We cannot expect to live a life of great joy and abundance with negative emotions and disobedience inside of us.

Love is described so many times and in so many ways in the New Testament, it can be said that the New Testament is the story of God's love for His people because He gave His only son for the remission of our sins. God loved us so much that He gave a piece of Himself for us. Love is the essence of the message in the New Testament. For instance, Galatians 5:16 says "For all he law is fulfilled in one word, even in this: You shall love your neighbor as yourself." In 1 Corinthians 13:13 Paul said, "Now abide faith, hope love, these three, but the greatest of these is love."

It's all about God and God is love. It's all about love. I never knew this before and now that I know, it has changed my life forever. God is so very good and faithful. His love provides so much to me; it comforts me and provides all my needs. I am never alone nor am I ever sad. If a believer has love, then things that concerned him will no longer cause him concern.

If you want abundance in your life, first want it for others (an expression of love) and if you want happiness in your life, then want it for others first (another expression of love). If we all allow God's love to flow through us and in us, we will live a truly extraordinary life. You will be able to move from a life of suffering to light, once you open up your core to love. Light begets light. Love begets love. Johann Wolfgang von Goethe said, "Light, light, the world needs more light."

Love cannot live alongside pride, ego, bitterness, anger, hatred, envy and other negative forces. Commit to love completely, love with your whole heart; and your life will explode with blessings and abundance. Love is the real secret to success. The Bible says love never fails.

The Happy Habit

Survey after survey has shown that it is unhappy people who tend to be most self-focused and are often socially withdrawn, brooding and even antagonistic. Happy people, in contrast, are generally found to be more sociable, flexible, and creative and are able to tolerate life's daily frustrations more easily than unhappy people. And most importantly, happy people are found to be more loving and forgiving than unhappy people.

Researchers have devised some interesting experiments demonstrating that happy people exhibit a certain quality of openness, a willingness to reach out and help others. I believe that even if we are not happy, if we participate in happy activities like going to church, volunteering and helping others without expectation of a reward, we can make ourselves happier. Genetic makeup plays a role in happiness and the verdict is still out how large that role is -- there is a general agreement among psychologists that no matter what level of happiness we are endowed with by nature, there are steps we can take to work out with the "mind factor" to enhance our feelings of happiness. This is because our moment to moment happiness is largely determined by our outlook. In fact, whether we are feeling happy or unhappy at any given moment often has very little to do with our absolute condition but rather it is a function of -- how we perceive our situation, how satisfied we are with what we have (The Art Of Happiness: A Handbook For Living page 22). During the worse time in my life, I was full of joy because I perceived my identity through Jesus Christ, knowing that God would never leave nor forsake me. I was grateful for life and knew the best was yet to come. My mood was stable and I was an encourager to those around me because I was balanced.

Our feelings of contentment are strongly influenced by our tendency to compare. Constant comparison with those who are smarter, more beautiful, or more successful than ourselves also tends to breed envy, frustration and unhappiness. We can increase our feeling of life satisfaction by comparing ourselves to those who are less fortunate that us and by reflecting on all the things we have.

Our mental outlook is the key to living a happy life. We all recognize there are several factors can assist in achieving a level of happiness such as good health, friendship and companionship but our state of mind is key. If we utilize our favorable circumstances such as our good health or wealth, in positive ways, in helping others, they can be contributory factors in achieving a happier life. And of course, we enjoy these things -- out material facilities, success and so on. But without the right mental attitude, without attention to the mental factor, these things have very little impact on our long-term feelings of happiness. For example, if you harbor hateful thoughts or intense anger somewhere deep down with yourself, then it ruins your health; thus it destroys one of the factors. Also, if you are mentally unhappy or frustrated, then physical comfort is not much help. On the other hand, if you can maintain a calm, peaceful state of mind, then you can be a very happy person even if you have poor health (The Art of Happiness: A Handbook for Living pages 24-25).

If you possess this inner quality, a calmness of mind, a degree of stability with, then even if you lack various external facilities that you would normally consider necessary for happiness, it is still possible to live a happy and joyful life (The Art of Happiness: A Handbook for Living page 26).

It's important to be content with what we have. The reliable method is not to have what we want but rather to want and appreciate what we have (The Art of Happiness: A Handbook for Living page 29).

Another internal source of happiness, closely linked with an inner feeling of contentment, is a sense of self-worth.

True happiness relates more to the mind and the heart. Happiness that depends mainly on physical pleasure is unstable; one day it's there, the next it may not be (The Art of Happiness: A Handbook for Living page 33).

We can train the mind for happiness. In identifying one's mental state as the prime factor in achieving happiness, of course that doesn't deny that our basic physical needs for food, clothing, and shelter must be met. But once these basic needs are met, the message is clear: we don't need more money, we don't need greater success or fame, we don't need the perfect body or even the perfect mate -- right now, at this very moment, we have a mind, which is all the basic equipment we need to achieve compete happiness (The Art of Happiness: A Handbook for Living page 37). I call this the "we are already fully equipped principle."

The first step in seeking happiness is learning. There is the realization of the beneficial aspects of maintaining positive emotions and behaviors. Once we realize that, we become determined to cherish, develop and increase those positive emotions no matter how difficult that is. We gradually develop a firm determination to change, feeling 'Now the secret to my own happiness, my own good fortune, is within my own hands. I must not miss this opportunity (The Art of Happiness: A Handbook for Living page 38). If you maintain a feeling of compassion, loving kindness, then something automatically opens your inner door. Through that, you can communicate much more easily with other people. And that feeling of warmth creates a kind of openness. You'll find that all human beings are just like you, so you'll be able to relate to them more easily.

If happiness is simply a matter of cultivating more positive mental states like kindness and so on, 'why are so many people unhappy?' Achieving genuine happiness may require bringing about a transformation in your outlook, you way of thinking, and this is not a simple matter, states the Dalai Lama. "It requires the application of so many different directions. You shouldn't have the notion, for instance, that there is just one key, a secret, and if you can get it right, then everything will be okay. ...Change takes time...transforming you mind takes time....But I thing that as time goes on, you can make positive changes. Every day as soon as you get up, you can develop a sincere positive motivation, thinking, 'I will utilize this day in a more positive way. I should not waste this very day.' And then at night before bed, check what you've done, asking yourself, 'Did I utilize this day as I planned?' If it went accordingly, then you should rejoice. If it went wrong, then regret what you did and critique that day. So through methods such as this, you can gradually strengthen the positive aspects of the mind (The Art of Happiness: A Handbook for Living pages 41-42).

The systematic training of the mind -- the cultivation of happiness, the genuine inner transformation by deliberately selecting and focusing on positive mental states and challenging negative mental states -- is possible because of the very structure and function of the brain. We are born with brains that are generically hardwired with certain instinctual behavior patterns; we are predisposed mentally, emotionally, and physically to respond to our environments in ways that enable us to survive. These basic sets of instructions are encoded in countless innate nerve cells activation patterns, specific combinations of brain cells that fire in response to any given event, experience, or thought. But the wiring in our brains is not static, not irrevocably fixed. Our brains are also adaptable. Neuroscientists have documented the fact that the brain can design new patterns, new combinations of nerve cells and neurotransmitters (chemicals that transmit messages between nerve cells) in response to new input. In fact, our brains are malleable, ever changing, reconfiguring their wiring according to new thoughts and experiences. And as a result of learning, the function of individual neurons themselves change, allowing electrical signals to travel along them more readily. Scientists call the brain's inherent capacity to change "plasticity" (from "The Art of Happiness, A Handbook for Living," Howard Cutler, M.D.; Riverhead Books, New York, 1998 pages 44-45.)

Remember, one can learn to be happy, but change takes time and a commitment and the Apostle Paul learned this point. We will delve into that in section two of this book.

Understanding life's trials

Kirk Franklin has an amazing Song called "Brighter Day". There are some lyrics in the song which have great meaning for me. "I never knew I could be so happy. I never knew that I'd be so secure but because of your love Jesus, life has brand new meaning. It's going to be a brighter day."

An amazing awakening can come from pain or trauma. Anyone can achieve a better life through accepting Jesus in their hearts. We have a choice, we can succumb to the pain, resentment, self-pity, bitterness which allows one to feel like a victim; or we can accept God's amazing grace and love. You can yield to the darkness or you can resist those negative emotions and become wiser, more forgiving, more compassionate and loving by embracing the light. It's our choice.

No one is immune to tragedy in this life. Being one with God is the goal which leads to that fulfillment. Every part of us must be working toward the same goal. So many people have a war going on inside of them.

We need to move from awareness to practical application. We should allow the information of the scriptures to become revelation in our heart, mind and soul through the Holy Spirit. The Bible says that faith without works is dead. It also says in James that we should be doers of the word instead of hearers only.

Jesus says in Mark 16:17-18,"... These signs shall follow them that believe; in my name shall they cast out devils; they shall speak with new tongues; ... they shall lay hands on the sick, and they shall recover." We can transform our lives by recalibrating our thoughts, words, and actions to the wisdom of the Bible.

The Lord's Prayer asks God to give us our daily bread. The model prayer taught to us by Jesus does not ask us for bread for next week or bread from last week. We are taught to ask for today's portion. When Moses and his people were in the wilderness, they received the manna from heaven each day. God advised them to only get the amount that they could eat that day. That is a powerful lesson to live an abundant life. We need to focus on enjoying every moment, being present in every moment.

Suffering comes when we stress over the future or relive painful moments from the past but if we focus on the present you will see that you have the conditions for your happiness in the present. The devil loves to torture us when we remember those painful memories of the past. The devil also loves when we become anxious over the uncertain future. The Bible tells us to not worry or be anxious for anything.

"Therefore do not worry about tomorrow, for tomorrow will worry about itself. Each day has enough trouble of its own (Matthew 6:34)."

We have the power to decide what we meditate on with our thoughts. We can choose thoughts which empower us and which honor God. We can choose to praise God or we can choose to complain. We can choose to focus on our blessings instead of focusing on our problems.

So many times in life we allow our insecurities to take the front seat. Our value is dependent on us being children of the Most High God. The Bible states in 1 John 4:6 that "we are of God." Many people are completely identified with that voice inside their heads, the nonstop stream of compulsive negative thoughts. Our thinking can be affected and influenced by aspects of past and the current negative programming in the word. That said, we have a choice.

Ultimately, we cannot be good to each other until we are good to ourselves; also and more importantly, we cannot love others until we love ourselves. Jesus was asked the greatest commandment. He says that we should love the Lord with all our heart, soul and mind, and the second one is that we should love our neighbors' as ourselves. So, we cannot love our neighbor if we do not know how to love ourselves.

Everyone's goal should be to re-wire their thinking patterns and live intentionally by choosing Godly thoughts. Our feelings can betray us because they are impulsive and reactive. We need to understand that life is an exercise with infinite outcomes. We cannot transform ourselves by making the same mistakes. Its only through change can we elevate ourselves. We must learn from our failures. Are you fulfilled? Are you happy with your life as it is? If not, then change it. If you want more than you have to put more into it. An open mind yields more possible positive results. A closed mind equals the same results.

When things fall apart, when your life falls apart, we should all praise God because its only through this process that we can put back together the pieces in the way we want. We can choose to put it back together in a whole and healthy way. Disaster can lead to the most amazing change that ever happened. My fall has allowed me to look inward in ways that I would never have contemplated previously. Out of crisis, comes opportunity. Christian enlightenment, mindfulness, consciousness over what I think and say are part of my default now.

We must live our Christ nature, a God-consciousness, thought consciousness, word consciousness. We were made to elevate ourselves. Jesus said, "Be perfect, therefore, as your heavenly Father is perfect (Matthew 5:48)." We have our goal in life, to be better than we were because we were born with a sinful nature. The Bible says that, "... for all have sinner and fall short of the glory of God (Romans 3:23)." We were given the opportunity to choose the type of life we want. We may have been marked by sin but we can reach up, strive forward to a greatness. God is perfect and sinless and thus cannot accept any type of sin from us. The wages of sin is death according to the Bible. In James 2:10, we learn that, "For whoever keeps the whole law and yet stumbles at just one point is guilty of breaking all of it. God cannot permit sin of any type to exist. But because God so loved the world that He gave His only begotten Son to pay for our sins so that we could have everlasting life (John 3:16).

Being angry, jealous, and self-obsessed leads to pain because they constrict the mind and make awareness more difficult. Meditating on compassionate and loving thoughts every morning helps to free us from ego and suffering.

What are you planting in your garden each day? Thoughts are like seeds, words are like the early sprouts and our actions/behaviors are what is reaped. A drop of poison put into an aquarium pollutes all the water and can kill the fish. Just like the verse in James 2:10, if we break one portion of law then we are guilty of breaking it all. So, in order to find our way, one needs to take the time to show love for themselves by doing things to enlighten oneself. It's a process, a process of faith. This process does not happen overnight but through a continued effort. No one achieves any success in a sport or profession without focus and dedication so this process requires the same focus, only inwardly.

As you start this new journey, here are 10 suggestions to empower you!

1) Raise you level of belief & expectation!

2) Change your inner & outer dialogue.

3) Examine yourself daily.

4) Determine what is your gift?

5) And which ability or gift will serve God & fulfill you.

6) Keep moving forward toward

the upward call of Christ Jesus.

7) Seek progress because progress equals joy.

8) See yourself as God sees you:

Loved, accepted, complete & whole

through the blood of Christ.

9) Strive to add light, value, kindness &

goodness each day to the world.

10) Always pursue love and seek peace!

The Battle

In combat zones, soldiers always pack their own ruck sacks. A ruck sack is a large back pack and it contains all one needs for the combat mission. Soldiers put MRE's (meals ready to eat), bivy-sac, sleeping bag, extra clothes in Ziploc bags, gas mask, atropine for chemical attacks and other things. Some things are mandatory but there were some things that soldiers put in which were optional such as extra socks, extra power bars, extra batteries, extra ammunition, and other non-essential gear which weigh down the soldier. No one tells the soldier what to pack in their ruck sack outside of the essentials. I use this as an analogy for life. Many of us carry around a lot in our ruck sack everyday such as emotional garbage from the past or regrets from the past or worries about the future which weigh us down. Some soldiers say that they would rather carry more gear which is a heavier load because they prefer to be comfortable at night. But it was their responsibility to carry their own ruck sack.

What are you carrying in your ruck sack daily?

Pain from old relationships, grudges from the past worries about the future, etc.? It's your choice what you decide to carry in your ruck sack. Is that junk from the past weighing you down? If so, you can refuse to carry it any longer.

Too many people fight the wrong battles. Instead of fighting the battle inside to tame their demons, they fight those around them because they are hurting. I know how it is to feel lost, be depressed and have no hope. I know how it feels to be hit so hard that all one wants to do is to stay on the ground and wish the pain away. I know what it feels like to be isolated from family and friends; and ridiculed from those who you thought cared about you. There was a direct correlation to how I lived my life and the pain which came into my life. My ruck sack was full of illusions, faulty beliefs and delusions.

Thus, when I started looking at changing to become a better, more God-conscious person, I had to clean out my ruck sack. I went through and learned that I was carrying past failure around and anxieties about the future that made it difficult for me to enjoy life on a daily basis by carrying as light a load as possible. I decided that I wanted to eject that garbage from the past.

My ruck sack is now very light because I live in the present. I make an effort to not let random thoughts nest in my mind for more than a brief moment. Once, I recognize a negative thought or a thought not pleasing to God - I recognize it for what it is and do not judge it – and then I change the channel in my head. I used to kick out the thoughts after judging it as bad. I am now mindful of what I think without judging it but maintain an awareness that the thought is not healthy before I move on. I now make an effort to live in the present moment while focusing on what is under my control (my thoughts). This allows me to be gentle with myself while I make changes toward being a more loving life with God at the center.

I know that it was only through the loss of my job that I even entertained the idea that I should change. I was very successful at my job. I thought failure was the end of my life. I did not know that failure could be the start of a greater second act. Failure is not final. By living through a loss or a tragedy, we can decide to start over with a new dream.

Too many Christians are "prisoners of war" of the devil and their own negative thinking. I just want to remind the reader that Jesus came to set the captives free. Luke 4:18 says clearly, The Spirit of the LORD is upon me, for he has anointed me to bring Good News to the poor. He has sent me to proclaim that captives will be released, that the blind will see, that the oppressed will be set free..."

Let go of the old image of yourself in order to be who God created you to be. It was only through letting go that we can achieve a transcendent shift. No more excuses or conditions. Why not do something different? I had felt that God was knocking on the outer recesses of my heart for so many years, but I always said, "not now, later." Are you saying the same thing to God? They say that tomorrow is not guaranteed to us.

It can be amazing once you decide to take a different path. You must want a changed life. I will break it down to an easy sentence:

God's desires and our response to His desires. It is simple. Stop fighting and receive the grace that God had been trying to give me for years. A better way, a smarter way, and a more peaceful way will ensue when you stop fighting Him.

God has a purpose for our failures or suffering; the key is to learn the lesson that God is trying to teach us. In accepting change and embracing a different path, I had to make an effort daily to work on a few specific spiritual principles to change my internal programming:

1. Be tolerant of those who are still living a defeated life in a fallen world. Not everyone will want the same gift of grace from God, just because you have received it. Thus, sow seeds of goodness and let you inner light show so brightly that others ask you how you found inner peace.

2. Stop being offended at the behavior of others, but instead get offended at your own behavior. In this vein, practice being patient

with those who are still trying to find their way. We all make choices in life and some will continue to bump into the walls.

3. Let everyone see the light and love inside of you. Look for the love and light in others. Continue to be humble so that others are attracted to what you are promoting.

4. Stay teachable. Always look to grow to higher levels. Strive to be more than you are.

5. Most importantly, eradicate any prideful feelings because of my own successful internal change. Pride ruined me before and will ruin me again if I do not stay tolerant, be patient, stay humble and teachable. Being a servant for Christ is about showing others how to find the light. Jesus washed the feet of His disciples. Jesus was not above being the love He promoted. My goal, be the love and light for others.

I love the story of Moses because his story is one of change. The first 40 years of his life was lived in luxury preparing to be Pharaoh. Moses was highly favored until he killed the Egyptian. Change was a necessity for Moses so he fled to Median where he became a shepherd for the next 40 years. It was only in the third part of his life when God stepped in that he found favor again. Moses accepted the grace from God. We all need to accept the grace of God because His saving grace is free. We must all try to glean the purpose of our specific trials, what is God trying to teach us?

I propose that change is essential to discover the God-ness in us because the world tends to reinforce our fallen nature. I believe that God allows us to fall or fail in order to experience the change necessary in order to be who He calls us to be. These are the reason that why I think God allows us to go through disasters:

1. To correct us of our mistakes like when Israel disobeyed God in the Old Testament book of Judges 2.

2. To educate us like in Joseph's case in Genesis.

3. To test our endurance like Job. It's a barometer to measure falsehoods, realities, and burn off the illusions/delusions we grow accustomed to through the conditioning.

4. To prepare us for greater attainment. Like in Moses' case, God was preparing Moses for greater things. Moses believed that the position of Pharaoh was the greatest position on the planet then. But today, most people do not even know the names of most pharaohs, but everyone in almost all religious traditions knows the name of Moses. Moses did not know what God had in store for him, but he trusted God. God has a destination for us all.

It's time to reveal the lies about ourselves! Defy all expectations!! Be the person who God and your inner self want you to be! There are eternal truths and when we follow the positive paths there are great rewards. When we follow the negative paths, there are great penalties.

James 1:17 states, "Every good and perfect gift is from above, coming down from the Father of heavenly lights, who does not change like shifting shadows." There was always that small still voice inside but I never listened to it. I had to change from the inside. Change was my ultimate goal after I started looking upward and inward. Religion should make us better, more loving and compassionate people.

It takes acknowledgement of and nurturing of God's presence on the inside, to change us on the outside. I learned that if I lived outside of God's will, then my life would be miserable. Joy and happiness is now possible once you turn your life over to God. God helped me to move from a place of despair to one of inner peace. The goodness of God made me whole again and it can do the same for you but you must make your religious practice real. Our religious practice must be real on the inside with God directing us our thoughts, words and actions. Our faith in Christ can heal any sickness, addiction or stronghold.

We get what we aim for in life but different goals get different results. I decided that I needed a life coach to help me through life. I decided the best life coach for me was Jesus Christ, His teachings and words.

Make Jesus Christ your life coach because He is the way, the truth and the life. Jesus is the only way to the Father and to everlasting life.

Being a joy-filled Christian includes fellowship

Jesus explained that the second part of the greatest commandment was to "Love your neighbor as yourself." Being a part of a spiritual community, a family of believers, is an important part of the joy-filled Christian.

"not forsaking the assembling of ourselves together, as *is* the manner of some, but exhorting *one another,* and so much the more as you see the Day approaching (Hebrews 10:25)."

Some people ask where is the church today with all the pain and suffering in the world. Let's define "who is the church?"

The church is the body of believers. We are the church, I am the church and you are the church.

In The Revelation of Jesus Christ, John records Jesus' words where He discusses the seven churches. I look at these seven churches as how I lived my life at various times but now I strive to be the faithful church (number 6). Can you identify yourself as one of the seven churches below?

1) The loveless church: the key verses are, "Nevertheless I have this against you that you have left your first love (Rev 2:4)." "He who has an ear, let him hear what the Spirit says the churches. To him who overcomes, I will give to eat from the tree of life, which is in the midst of the Paradise of God (Rev 2:7)." Love is the basis of the Christian walk and we need to be stirred up, and return to our first love - God.

2) The persecuted church: the key verses are, "Do not fear any of those things which you are about to suffer. Indeed, the devil is about to throw some of you into prison, that you may be tested, and you will have tribulation ten days. Be faithful until death, and I will give you the crown of life. He who has an ear, let him hear what the Spirit

says to the churches. He who overcomes shall not be hurt by the second death (Rev 2:10-11). Tribulations are to be expected and if we stay faithful, we will reap in due time.

3) The compromising church: the key verses are, "But I have a few things against you, because you have there those who hold the doctrine of Balaam, who taught Balak to put stumbling blocks before the children of Israel, to eat things sacrificed to idols, and to commit sexual immorality (Rev 2:14)." "He who has an ear, let him hear what the Spirit says to the churches. To him who overcomes I will give some of the hidden manna to eat. I will give him a white stone, and on the stone a new name written which no one knows except him who receives it (Rev 2:17)." Too many people compromise in life, moving further away each day from God's system in favor of the system of men. Everyone stumbles or backslides from time to time, but the Christian is about getting back up, repenting and then moving forward. "Godly sorrow brings repentance that leads to salvation and leaves no regret, bit worldly sorrow brings death (2nd Corinthians 7:10)."

4) The corrupt church: the key verses are, "Nevertheless I have a few things against you, because you allow that woman Jezebel, who calls herself a prophetess to teach ad seduce My servants to commit sexual immorality and eat things sacrificed to idols. And I gave her time to repent to her sexual immorality, and she did not repent. Indeed I will cast her into a sickbed, and those who commit adultery with her into great tribulation, unless they repent of their deeds (Rev 2:20-22)." "But hold fast what you have till I come. And he who overcomes, and keeps My works until the end, to him I will give power over nations (Rev 2:25-26)." Many of us are our own worst enemies (like I was to myself until my eyes opened), bringing on destruction on ourselves by the decisions we make. But God will allow us to repent and return back into union with Him through Jesus Christ.

5) The dead church: the key verses are, "Be watchful and strengthen the things which remain, that are ready to die, for I have not found your works perfect before God. Remember therefore how you received and heard; hold fast and repent. Therefore if you will not watch, I will come upon you as a thief, and you will not know what

hour I will come upon you (Rev 3:2-3)." "He who overcomes shall be clothed in white garments, and I will not blot out his name before My Father and before the angels (Rev 3:5)." There is such great wisdom in the above verse that it needs no explanation.

6) The faithful church: the key verses are," I know your works. See, I have set before you an open door and no one can shut it, for you have a little strength, have kept My word and have not denied my name (Rev 3:8)." "Because you have kept My command to persevere, I also will keep you from the hour of trial which shall come upon the whole world, to test those who dwell on earth. Behold, I am coming quickly Hold fast what you have, that no one may take your crown. he who overcomes, I will make him a pillar in the temple of My God, and he shall go out no more. I will write on him the name of My God, and the name of the city of My God, the New Jerusalem, which comes down out of heaven from My God. And I will write on him my new name (Rev 3:10-12)." This is the church I am trying to imitate. I have been a part of all the churches mentioned here but now I strive to be faithful. We are God's greatest masterpiece, the crown is already yours, do not let anyone take your

crown. I have traveled to Jerusalem and I want to see the New Jerusalem. I also strive today to have a new name. Is this the church you are striving to be?

7) The Lukewarm church: the key verses are, "I know your works, that you are neither cold not hot. I could wish you were cold or hot. SO then, because you are lukewarm, and neither cold nor hot, I will vomit you out of my mouth (Rev 3:15-16)." "As many as I love, I rebuke and chasten. Therefore be zealous and repent. Behold, I stand at the door and knock. If anyone hears My voice and opens the door, I will come in to him and dine with him, and he with Me. To him who overcomes, I will grant to sit with Me on My throne, as I also overcame and sat down with My Father on His throne. (Rev 3:19-21)." I don't wish Jesus to vomit me out of his mouth. I used to be lukewarm but now I am on fire for God! I have seen the light and ever fiber on my being strives each day to stay in the light. I am an overcomer and you are an overcomer!

Which church are you? I never understood the above passage before but now I see that through my life I have exhibited traits from each one. I never understood that I had a choice. God is so good and merciful, Oh how I love Him because he saved a sinner like me. Try Him, he is faithful and wants all of us to prosper which is why we have his Words to help guide us to live an abundant life! Ask yourself this day, am I doing all I can for God?

Rejoice! For today you have a choice to return back to God, stir up the gifts that he has been given to you. Be passionate for God! I invite you to read Revelations chapters two and three so that you can be moved by the words of Jesus, as they moved me. I encourage you this day to get excited about serving God! God is in your corner, and loves you unconditionally!

Life in Christ involves constantly seeking God's purpose for our lives. It's important that we are part of a community and regular church attendance helps to fill the believer with joy.

"Then the children of Israel who had returned from the captivity ate together with all who had separated themselves from the filth of the nations of the land in order to seek the LORD God of Israel. [22] And they kept the Feast of Unleavened Bread seven days with joy; for the LORD made them joyful, and turned the heart of the king of Assyria toward them, to strengthen their hands in the work of the house of God, the God of Israel (Ezra 6:21-22)."

Take joy and make joy a daily habit!

Faith as a major habit in our daily walk

It says, "Abraham believed God, and that faith was regarded by God to be his approval of Abraham." So Abraham was called God's friend. And that the scripture was fulfilled which saith, Abraham believed God, and it was imputed unto him for righteousness, and he was called the Friend of God.

One of my favorite songs in the hymnal is "What a Friend We Have in Jesus." Without reservation, we readily admit that Jesus is a friend to us! But have you ever seriously considered what it means to be a friend to Him?

You might be surprised to know that the Bible provides examples and specific principles to help us understand exactly how to be a friend of God.

1. A friend of God is one who values His presence above all else.

Moses had spent the last forty days alone with God. While there he had received both the law and the rules of worship from God. Imagine his dismay when, upon his return to the camp, he found the people engaged in idolatrous worship and licentious behavior! In fact, were it not for the intercession of Moses, God would have destroyed His people right there in the wilderness.

As it turned out, the Lord refused to lead them any further by His presence. From now on He would merely use an angel to direct their journey.

But Moses refused to accept such a proposition. If the Lord did not travel with them, Moses was staying put! (See Exodus 33:15.) In fact, the conversation Moses shared with the Lord revealed Moses' supreme desire to know God intimately.

And the LORD spake unto Moses face to face, as a man ***speaketh unto his friend***. And he turned again into the camp: but his servant Joshua, the son of Nun, a young man, departed not out of the tabernacle.—Exodus 33:11

More than he wanted the Promised Land with all its prospects of stability and fruitfulness, Moses wanted the presence of Almighty God.

Friends of God are they who prioritize their relationship with Him, not allowing the work of God ever to replace the God of the work in their devotion.

2. A friend of God will live a life of faith.

At the foundation of every healthy relationship is trust. Perhaps the greatest expression of my friendship with you is that I trust you no matter what.

Abraham is best noted for his faith in God; in fact, he has been called, "The Father of Faith."

And the scripture was fulfilled which saith, Abraham believed God, and it was imputed unto him for righteousness: and he was called **the Friend of God.**—James 2:23

Never forget that it is faith that pleases God (Hebrews 11:6). Abraham believed that God would make of him a great nation even when his wife was barren and beyond childbearing years. All he had to go on was the explicit Word of God. Circumstances, biology, and human reasoning shouted their objections to Abraham's faith.

What has God clearly said to you in His Word that you refuse to put into practice? Perhaps it is tithing, or soul winning, or extending forgiveness. Friends of God take Him at His Word. They know that God would never ask them to do something that was not mutually beneficial. Because Abraham believed God he was given the timeless label, "Friend of God" (2 Chronicles 20:7; Isaiah 41:8).

3. A friend of God is one who joyfully seeks His benefit and advances His agenda.

John the Baptist taught us a great lesson in the waning moments of his public ministry. His own disciples complained that the new ministry of Jesus Christ had eclipsed their own both in popularity and in the sheer number of those baptized. To adjust their carnal thinking, John employed the illustration of a friend—a best man.

He that hath the bride is the bridegroom: but the *friend of the bridegroom*, which standeth and heareth him, rejoiceth greatly because of the bridegroom's voice: this my joy therefore is fulfilled.—John 3:29

Your true friend would rather that you bask in the limelight, that you receive the compliment, and that you enjoy the credit. The closer one's relationship with God, the less he will be concerned about personal recognition.

It is enough for God's friends—and supremely satisfying to them—that God receives the glory! Examine your own heart—is that desire true of you?

4. A friend of God will carefully guard his affections and amusements.

Some friendships simply cannot exist simultaneously.

Ye adulterers and adulteresses, know ye not that the friendship of the world is enmity with God? whosoever therefore will be a friend of the world is the enemy of God.—James 4:4

Wickedness and worship cannot coexist. Friends of God are those whose love for God transcends the allure of a world system with its concomitant lusts and pride (1 John 2:15-17).

Am I a friend of the world or a friend of God? Review your schedule and your priorities. They will tell you the truth about your friendships.

5. A friend of God is privy to special information and is supremely reliable with it.

Think for a moment about your closest friends. They are the ones with whom you can share even the most confidential information. You trust them and know that they will always act in your best interest.

Humanly speaking, the best friends of Jesus were His disciples. With them He shared His deepest thoughts, emotions, and visions. To them He carefully provided instruction and expectation.

Greater love hath no man than this, that a man lay down his life for his *friends*. *Ye are my friends*, if ye do whatsoever I command you. Henceforth I call you not servants; for the servant knoweth not what his lord doeth: but *I have called you friends*; for all things that I have heard of my Father I have made known unto you.—John 15:13-15

Joy and peace connected as the second and third fruit of the Spirit. Galatians 6:22 states, "But the fruit of the Spirit is love, joy, peace, longsuffering, kindness, goodness, faithfulness,[23] gentleness, self-control. Against such there is no law."

Jesus tells us, "Peace I leave with you, Do not let your hearts to be troubled (John 14:27)."

"Peace I leave with you, My peace I give to you; not as the world gives do I give to you. Let not your heart be troubled, neither let it be afraid (John 14:27)."

The Bible gives us much peace because it gives us amazing promises which we can hold onto during the storms in our lives. Joy comes not from our circumstances but knowing that God will never leave nor forsake us. Trust God to do His part while we focus on doing our part.

"Finally, brethren, whatever things are true, whatever things are noble, whatever things are just, whatever things are pure, whatever things are lovely, whatever things are of good report, if there is any virtue and if there is anything praiseworthy—meditate on these things (Philippians 4:8)."

Joy also comes through the listening while we mediate on God's word. In the midst of our electronic generation of instant communication, information, and entertainment, is anyone listening to God? He wants to communicate with us and has been speaking ever since creation. In the Old Testament, He spoke through prophets; in the New Testament, through His Son (Heb. 1:1-2). He continues communicating now through the Holy Spirit (John 16:13). The issue is not whether God is speaking, but whether we are listening.

When we listen, He'll guide us and provide what we truly need:

To make decisions. Because God is interested in every aspect of our lives, He wants to guide each choice we make.

To be encouraged. No one can encourage our hearts like the Lord, but we have to listen to Him, or we'll miss it.

To receive comfort. Sometimes we just need to be reminded that He loves us unconditionally and is always ready to help us through difficult circumstances.

To be strengthened. Whenever we need the will, determination, and confidence to keep going, God can strengthen us.

To know the Father's will. When we're seeking to understand His will, we must stop talking and listen to hear His voice.

To receive God's best. The Lord always does what's best when we heed His instructions.

To have assurance of salvation. The only way to silence doubts is to listen to the Lord. He saved us once for all time and eternity.

To benefit from His protection. When we follow the Lord's guidance and make good choices, He protects us from wrong relationships and activities.

The habit of loving and accepting the life that God has given us

Life for some can becomes a perpetual struggle for more; I want, I need. This is because we have not learned to control our thoughts. Everyone has the possibility to allow their thoughts to run wild. We become a slave to every fleeting thought but once we become more disciplined with our thoughts, peace follows. I, like many people, was trapped in bad habits of my likes and dislikes. Suffering comes from a subtle sense of unsatisfactoriness; we think that we don't have enough. God has a perfect love for us. Each of us need to stop identifying themselves with exterior factors. We each have all the conditions for our own happiness right now. It's time to get off that mental treadmill of hashing and rehashing every little issue in our lives over and over. Move your thoughts to more spiritual topics.

Too many people believe once that get "XYZ" then they will be happy. We are always craving something. We are never satisfied. I was on this same mental treadmill wanting more things. Many people have no idea of who they are, their lives have no meaning or purpose. We all struggle to find our purpose. We each have an overdeveloped sense of the material aspect of the world and an underdeveloped sense of the deeper spiritual aspect of the world. All of us need to purify our minds and ask God to burn off all the impurities in us.

Here is what is going on inside most people's minds: "I want, I need, I feel, he or she did this or that to me" but this is part of the illusion. Erase the blinders which have diverted you from your destiny. I have all I need right now and it's because of God love. Look inward. God is love and I am to love Him and others--enough said!

Google analytics reveals that the word "porn" is googled 20 times more than the word "Jesus". Most self-identified Christians (54%) do not pick up a Bible on a weekly basis. The most popular day to view pornography on the internet is Sunday. The word "sex" is googled 15 times more than the word "God". Only 2 out of 10 Christians volunteer at church. Just look at how many Christians at your church attend bible study on a regular basis.

This country's own appetites reveal ourselves to us. The devil works hard to keep us down. The evil one knows what we like and hot to tempt us. This is why it's so important to have a solid spiritual base and to be aware of what's going on inside our internal world. If you look deeply inside yourself, you will find your feelings are responsible for all the conflict in your life. Being conscious and aware of everything we do or think can break those chains that had us bound for many years.

In my studies over the last few years, I learned some interesting things about how people intellectualized or play intellectual games with their religion to make it work for them. Religion (and I mean religion in context with a deep relationship with Jesus) is supposed to change us, so that we become better people. Religion should bring about salvation, liberation, an inner freedom, happiness and joy. Religion should make us better, healthier people spiritually. Spiritual healthy brings about overall heath. We all have been polluted in how we think. We fall for situational insanity and maintain defective relationships with others and with ourselves. Our minds are naturally undisciplined; thus it will take some training to control our mind.

Learned insanity should not be continued. We need to dissolve the beliefs of the past. Examine yourself, to know yourself. Allow the Holy Spirit into your heart and He will make a radical change in your thinking. As new creatures in Christ, the believer's mind has an unimaginable capacity to adapt and change. We are the ones who put our own selves in a box. We limit ourselves.

In 2 Peter 3:11, "Therefore since all these things will be dissolved, what manner of person ought you to be in holy condition and Godliness." I decided to start over inside to become the man I always wanted to be, and the man God wanted me to be. Radically change your life by changing your thoughts. Move closer to God.

The above verse shows me that all things are temporary, all things fade. Change is the only natural concept we can count on. In the above verse, there is a challenge. We have the power and we can accept the challenge or not. I pray each day that God help me become the person God He desires me to be. Life can be painful and involves change but only a close, personal relationship with God will provide an anchor.

Proverbs 4:23 states, "Be careful how you think; your life is shaped by your thoughts." If we think abundance always, see abundance everywhere, feel abundance daily and believe abundance will enter our lives, it will. Harness the power inside of yourself. Chaos inside of us, will always create chaos on the outside of us. We need to stop the learned patterned madness from our past conditioning.

In the Alcohol Anonymous (AA) book, there is a statement which says that they believe that *'nearly every serious emotional problem can be seen as a case of misdirected instinct.'* When that happens, our great natural assets, the instincts, have turned into physical or mental liabilities. We learn that step four is a *'vigorous and painstaking effort to discover what these liabilities in each of us have been, and are.'* We want to find exactly, how, when, and where our natural desires have warped us. We wish to look squarely at the unhappiness that has caused others and ourselves. It's through this practice that one can start to change and heal. Step 11 in AA is also a transformational step as it says, 'sought through prayer and meditation to improve our conscious contact with God as we understood Him, praying only for knowledge of His will for us and the power to carry that out." Later in the AA 12 step book, we learn that, *'there is a direct linkage among self-examination, meditation, and prayer. Taken separately, these practices can bring much relief and benefit. But when they are logically related and interwoven, the result is an unshakable foundation for life.'* If we seek, we will find it; but too few people execute a daily plan for their happiness. We have to trust the process whether following a 12 step program or reading the Bible. Too many people know what to do, but fail in the execution phase.

The revolution is supposed to take place inside of us. If we change first, then we can change the world. The Apostle Paul wrote some of the most amazing God inspired words. In Romans 8:18 we learn, "For I consider that the sufferings of this present time are not worthy to be compared with the glory which shall be revealed to us." Paul recognized that suffering occurred in this world just as the Buddha recognized the same fact. Each realized that transformation was possible.

Joy is the 2nd fruit of the Spirit. Joy encompasses cheerfulness, delight, and gladness which is not determined by our circumstances, but is a constant quality in every situation whether good or bad, because of our foundation in Godly living and thinking. The Apostle Paul wrote his amazing epistle to the Philippians when he was in a Roman prison. The epistle or letter is known as the 'joy letter'. In Philippians 4:11-12, Paul states from prison, "I have learned to be content in any and every situation." Paul was in prison awaiting for judgment. His source of contentment was the Holy Spirit and his relationship with Jesus Christ.

There is a strong connection between suffering and joy. Often we may not recognize the joy we have in our current lives until we face a tragedy. Once we have a spiritual awakening after suffering, we realize that we had the power all the time. Joy is not dependent on our circumstances but is a state emanating from within. For example, in the movie, The Wizard of OZ, Dorothy realizes at the end of the movie after all of her suffering that she always had the power to go home. We all have that power as well, we just have to realize it.

Some passages on joy and suffering:

--"Consider it pure joy, my brothers, whenever you face trials of many kinds, because you know that the testing of your faith develops perseverance (James 1:2)."

--"As you know, we consider blessed those who have persevered (James 5:11)."

--"But rejoice that you participate in the sufferings of Christ, so that you may be overjoyed when his glory is revealed (1 Peter 4:13)."

--"You sympathized with those in prison and joyfully accepted the confiscation of your property, because you knew that you yourselves had better and lasting possessions (Hebrews 10:34)."

--"In spite of severe suffering, you welcomed the message with the joy given by the Holy Spirit (Thessalonians 1:6)."

You can learn to live a different life, an inspired life. I love the verses in Romans 8:25-28, "But if we hope for what we do not see, we eagerly wait for it with perseverance. Likewise, the Spirit also helps in our weaknesses. For we do not know what we should pray for as we ought, but the Spirit Himself makes intercession for us with groanings which can't be uttered. Now, He who searches the hearts knows what the mind of the Spirit is, because He makes intercession for the saints according to the will of God. And we know that all things work together for good to those who love God, to those who are called according to His purpose."

God has a purpose for all of us. God wants us to have an amazingly abundant life!! God is our greatest cheerleader and wants us to be great.

In the Old Testament, God called the Israelites stiff-necked because they were so stubborn in their ways. We are just the same; stiff-necked in our ways. God had a cure for those stiff-necked and stubborn people in the Old Testament. Today, the difference is that we have a savior in Jesus Christ which makes the path easier than those Hebrews had it.

It's all about having faith. So many say they believe and have faith but their thoughts, words, and actions show that this is clearly not the case. Is this you? I could not answer this question in the affirmative before but now I have a fire inside to do God's will.

Faith is the great theme played out in the Bible. In Romans 1:17 we learn, "The righteous shall live by faith." In 2 Corinthians 5:7, "we live by faith, not sight." "Faith is the foundation of our relationship to God through His Son." The Bible contains many promises from God but we can't obtain these promises through half-hearted faith or belief. God wants some prayer and faith warriors. Is that you? I could not answer this question in the affirmative but now I put God first.

Because of the sin of unfaithfulness, the Israelites I mentioned above were finally taken into captivity. We all must remember, myself included, that "... a faithful man will be richly blessed (Proverbs 28:20)." I believe that we all want to hear God tell us one day, "Well done, good and faithful servant (Mathew 25:21)."

Man was created full of spiritual, mental, physical, and emotional energy which must be used properly and controlled in order to be beneficial to society. Thus, this energy must be harnessed through the Spirit of the Holy Ghost. Everything I am suggesting deals with allowing the Holy Spirit to change us.

When we allow the Holy Spirit to go to work on the inside of us, we can bring our mind and body under discipline through the ninth fruit of the Spirit of self-control. Once I became saved and the Holy Spirit started dwelling inside of me, I was no longer under the bondage of my sinful nature. It was only through study, prayer, loving, hoping, and living a self-disciplined life that I was able to live a more Christ-like life.

The information for spiritual salvation, inner peace, and joy is free and freely available for those who want it. Carl Jung stated that *"Knowing your own darkness is the best method of dealing with the darkness in other people."* Once I realized that we were all the same; compassion and love began to flow freely to others. We are all broken and all have the power to find the true path. The knowledge is not a secret, it's out there for all those who want it but many people don't. Once I gave my life to God, life became so much easier

"A very large amount of human suffering and frustration is caused by the fact that many men and women are not content to be the sort of beings that God has made them, but try to persuade themselves that they are really beings of some different kind." Eric Mascall, lecturer in Philosophy of Religion, Christ Church, Oxford.

Part II

The Joy-Filled Christian

Jesus says, "I tell you that in the same way, there will be more joy in Heaven over one sinner who repents than over ninety-nine righteous persons who need no repentance. (Luke 15:7)"

Every day, we all have a job to do--be a light to others. Jesus says in John 8:12, "I am light of the world. He who follows Me shall not walk in darkness, but have the light of life." I do my job by having joy in my heart and a smile on my face from the moment I wake up until I sleep. I choose to love; show love, express love and be love. It is a choice I have each day. It's the same choice that you have each day. My joy comes from the joy of the Lord which resides inside of me.

Tell yourself that the world cannot fill your heart with joy and the world cannot take it away.

The principles in the New Testament is like a business plan for us humans, "the human potential business." The business of helping people reach their potential. We should each strive to reach our potential.

We all suffer from the condition of being human and from being improperly programmed. It takes a long term focused plan to recover from the conditioning of the past.

We all have the following choices each day:

1) How to react to every situation which confronts us.

2) What meaning we want to attach to those situations.

God gives us the choice. We can carry 20 pounds of past baggage with us or we can choose to start each day anew, full of joy and hope.

"What time is it?

It's time to stop letting your past control your destiny.

Whatever evil that has bound you up in the past, I ask you to say out loud right now, "*In the name of God, I rebuke any evil spirits ever spoken over me. Abundance will now enter my life. I choose life and the light!*"

Sadness or depression cannot enter a heart full of joy and thankfulness. If you fill your heart with love, joy and gratefulness for all your blessings each day then the darkness will have a difficult time getting in.

I heard a person once say that crisis is a part of everyone's life: 1) we are either just going into a crisis; or 2) we are currently in a crisis; or 3) we are just moving out of a crisis.

Where are you?

Because of this phenomena, many people stay in crisis mode, all the time. Some people are addicted to crisis. The three above points are insightful regarding crisis but when one is whole and healthy, the crisis does not have a place to grow. Now, I have very few crisis, because my life is for the Lord and I see things differently now. The crisis you may be in right now may be the greatest learning opportunity in your life because you can grow, gain insight and actually find meaning and purpose from it.

Perspective is everything in life. Christians should have a Christ-focused perspective. We must tend to our own gardens, or they will become overgrown. There is no guilt or condemnation when one is in Christ. Under the blood of Jesus Christ, our sins are wiped clean and we become a new person. As a new person, we have a new job which is to bring others to the light, to show others that they have options in life. I never knew how many options I had in my life before I entered into a person and intimate relationship with Christ. I choose to have joy now.

I need to explain that just because I choose joy now, that does not mean that I never have a bad day. I just choose to focus on my blessings instead of my worries. I still have issues and problems in my life but I just don't worry as much anymore because I gave my life to Christ and have cast my cares on God. My perspective have changed and my goals have changed. My aim now is on things on high in God's kingdom.

My perspective is now centered on God. I know God loves and accepts me as I am. God loves and accepts you as well. God forgives us. Once we repent and turn away from our former sins, we are new creations in Christ, and we must live that way.

I thank God each day because of the blessing He places in my life. I never saw the need to thank God for waking me up each day. I never viewed life as a gift and I took that gift for granted. I am a former sinner redeemed by the blood of Christ who now wants to be a servant of God. I want to spread God's message and show others that even the most broken people can change and be used by God. "God heals the brokenhearted (Psalms 147:3)." God wants to help us empty our minds of negative thoughts and He will help us fill our minds with fresh thoughts of joy, faith, hope and goodness.

"Do not be grieved, for the joy of the Lord is your strength (Nehemiah 8:10)."

"Watch, stand fast in the faith, be brave, be strong. Let all that you do be done with love (1 Corinthians 16:13-14)."

We must not lose heart. I still make mistakes but I lean on God and get right back up without beating myself up. I repent my bad decisions now and make sure that I do not live in willful sin. I make decisions today looking at things through a God-consciousness.

Ask yourself daily: Are my actions daily pleasing to God or not?

Some people have forgotten how to be thankful, to enjoy life's little's blessings. People have been beaten down so much that they only know how to complain, hate, be derisive, ridicule or grumble. The energy used to live this way is a powerful negative force in those people's lives. I have found out where joy is: it's in Jesus Christ and it's inside me. We reap what we sow; so please choose to sow seeds of happiness each day.

Some people go through life believing they can barely make it. They see the world as one full of problems. They speak difficulty into their lives as they tumbles through the waves of life. These people just exist. But God! God does not wish that His people live this way. These people are like a leaf in the wind, they are blown around not understanding the power God has given them.

In Psalm 1:3, God describes the type of life he wants His people to live, "A tree planted by the rivers of water, that bringeth forth His fruit in His season; your leaf also shall not wither; and whatsoever you do shall prosper." If we live by God's word, it will be like the tree obtaining its nourishment from the riverbed. When the winds blow, its roots are strong and it may bend but it will not break, it will be steadfast because it had been made strong from the life giving water. God's word is the same yesterday, today and tomorrow. God's word can help you when the winds of depression or sorrow come on.

We need to be passionate about the word of God and passionate about living for the Lord. God is passionate about His people, and sends messages to us all the time but most times we allow the worldly things in our daily life to drown out that little still voice.

Psychologists say that an abnormal reaction to an abnormal situation is normal behavior. One acts in an abnormal fashion in proportion to the degree of his/her conditioning or programming. Some people love chaos which creates certain conditions in their life. Chaos brings chaos, but God is a game changer and does not operate as humans do. Faith can move mountains and just because one may be in an abnormal situation and that does not mean that your reaction to that situation has to be abnormal or un-Christlike.

Some thrive and are awakened through abnormal circumstances, learning a greater consciousness while growing more compassionate, less ego driven while others are still on the devil's merry go-round. I was awakened through my experience.

People have a passion for many worldly things, but if we have a passion for God, doors will appear that you could never have imagined. There are different doorways or paths one can choose, too many of us voluntarily choose pain. We do not have to be led by our negative feelings and random destructive thoughts. I have a God consciousness now which means I have a Word consciousness about what I say; and a thought consciousness about what I think. I am conscious about what I allow my mind to dwell on. Awareness is possible but it takes work, hard work. God said, "My people are destroyed for lack of knowledge (Hosea 4:6)." Joy and enthusiasm is the key. If we switch to praise, have an attitude of gratitude, stay positive and look for God's lessons in everything that happens to us, we will not only survive but thrive.

Henry Davis Thoreau said that *"Go confidently in the direction of your dreams."* When we align our intentions with God's, we can do just that!

You are good enough and loved by God who accepts you unconditionally

Many people struggle with feelings of being "not good enough." You are good enough and God loves you right now as much as He will always love you. Of course, we can disappoint God but God's love is always there, a constant. We are born, then raised and conditioned by our parents. After that period, we are socialized and conditioned by those around us and through the formal education process. Many people are mis-educated from an early age and then start to internalize certain negative thoughts and feelings. Jean-Jacques Rousseau said that, "*man is born free, and everywhere he is in chains.*" This statement describes what confronts people all the time, they limit themselves and believe in the illusions which often end with them thinking that they aren't good enough.

"The Lord says, 'You are precious and honored in My sight....Do not be afraid, for I am with you.'" (Isaiah 43:4-5).

Psalm 8:5 says, "Yet you have made them (humans) a little lower than God, and crowned them with glory and honor." By knowing and internalizing these simple scriptures, you can change your life by seeing yourself as God sees you.

From the time we are born to growing up, we develop a veil of perception over time, or I should say a veil of misperception. David Hume wrote in A treatise of Human Nature, *"...When I enter most intimately into what I call myself, I always stumble on some particular perception or other, of heat or cold, light or shade, love or hatred, pain or pleasure. I never can catch myself at any time without a perception, and never can observe anything but the perception."* This section is about changing one's perception so that everyone believes that they are good enough. Many people live a self-destructive lifestyle because deep down they do not feel they are worthy of love from God or from anyone else. You are worthy and deserving of love!

1 Peter 2:9 says, "But you are a chosen generation, a royal priesthood, a holy nation, His own special people, that you may proclaim the praises of Him who called you out of darkness into His marvelous light." This is a particularly interesting verse because it discusses who we are and how God sees us. The above verse also discusses the light and darkness. Being born in this world of sin and darkness, many people (myself included before I discovered a better way) succumb to the darkness believing that the darkness is where they are supposed to dwell.

In the Gospel of John 8:12, Jesus said, "I am the light of the world: he that follows me shall not walk in darkness, but shall have the light of life." These two verses explain that there is a better way. With that light before us, we have a guide and target to aim for. When we walk in His light our way is clear and our burdens are lighter but when we turn away from Him, then we walk in darkness, the darkness of our own shadow.

The darkness is the struggle within. Satan loves the darkness and is the father of lies. He wants us to believe that we have no choice but to live and stumble around in the darkness. Satan wants you to believe that you are not good enough for God's love. Satan wants you to believe you have no choice in the matter that once you are in the darkness you must stay there.

The great English philosopher Bertrand Russell said, "*There lies before us, if we choose, continual progress in happiness, knowledge, and wisdom. Shall we, instead, choose death.*"

In Deuteronomy 30:15-19, God says, "See I have set before you today life and good, death and evil,...I call heaven and earth as witnesses today against you that I have set before you life and death, blessing and cursing; therefore choose life, that both you and your descendants may live." God asks us to choose life. The light is already in us but because of the conditioning process, our internal

GPS leads us astray. When God asks us to choose life, I take this to mean that we should also choose an internal perspective which is pleasing to God.

Psalms 32:8 says, "I will instruct you and teach you in the way you should go; I will guide you with My eye." The better way I have come to follow did not come from me but from God.

We all fall short of the glory of God and we have all sinned according to the Bible. We should not use that as an excuse to wallow in a pool of self-pity or not strive to be better. Everyone will fall short from time to time but the important thing is to keep moving forward without beating oneself up. Each time, we fail its one step closer to success.

In each failure, there are lessons which can help us. Moving forward can only happen if our vision is clear and we maintain clarity of thought. 1 Corinthians 6:19 says, "Do you not know that your body is the temple of the Holy Spirit who is in you, whom you have from

God, and you are not your own." The Holy Spirit is already in us and we are God's property. God takes care of His property and have a vested interest in making sure we know the way. The path has been placed before us and we can all reach it through partnering with the Holy Spirit.

We can be move towards perfection by knowing that we are loved and are already good enough for God. Now, the job is to balance our desire for real change with our thoughts, words and actions which reflects that we believe we are good enough. James 2:20 says that, "...faith without works is dead." Many people stay in the muck because they do not understand who they are or the power they have inside. In Luke 17:20-21 states, "...For the kingdom of God is within you."

Jesus states in Matthew 5:16, Let your light shine before men in such a way that they may see your good works, and glorify your Father who is heaven." The verses are about knowing who you are. 1 John

4:4 states, "You are of God, little children, and have overcome them, because He who is in you is greater than he who is in the world."

Two verses later we read, "We are of God." Inside of us is a piece of God, waiting to come out and be activated through our efforts. Paul wrote in Romans 12:2, "Do not be conformed to this world, but be transformed by the renewing of your mind, that you may prove what is good and acceptable and perfect will of God."

When we internalize our brokenness, we tell the world that we are not good enough. Faith and fear cannot operate together. When we fear, doubt or otherwise lack faith, we are thinking. Fear and doubts are thoughts; negative thoughts leading to defeat. When you give into that type of thinking, you are telling yourself that you are not worthy.

After we are born, we start to create various mental schemas of how we see the world. I am proposing that you destroy those old schemas and create new schemas from light and love. Plato said, *"He whom love touches, walks not in darkness."* A deeper understanding of love leads to a new way of viewing the world. In our own imagination are the seeds for a better life.

"We perceive things not as they are but as we are", this quote accurately describes how many people go through life believing that they are less than worthy. William Blake stated in 'Jerusalem', "*I must create a system, or be enslaved by another man's; I will not reason and compare: my business is to create*." I love this statement because we are all looking for meaning and purpose in life and must create a system to acquire it. The Bible provides all wisdom we will ever need in life. I hope this works inspires you to develop your inner God-consciousness. I want you to know that you are already good enough already.

I discovered that I did not have to fill that inner void with accomplishments or through other means. I put my faith in the wrong things. It takes courage to believe in something that you can't see but I do. It takes courage to not follow the herd. It takes courage to stand up in the face of sickness and declare you are healed by the stripes of Jesus. It takes courage to dance and smile with real inner joy when you don't feel like it.

Everyone should believe that they are already good enough. In that same vein, you should know that life in this age can create a type of mental or spiritual sicknesses. Recovery is possible when your new focus is centered on faith in God. Even so, there will be challenges from all directions. Now with these challenges, your tool box is more prepared because you have a different perspective, a different internal focus where the things that bothered you previously will no longer be an issue. You will be challenged and people will attempt to get you off your new path. Once you have found the path, your goal is now to stay there and move along the path for further insights.

The battle of faith is not just fought once and then forgotten. The battle is constant and we must get up each morning focused on maintaining our spiritual foundation. Each day, we must lace up our boots and prepare ourselves for the trials, challenges and heartbreaks while understanding that God wants you to succeed and have an abundant life. You must understand God wants you to have inner joy. God wants to guide you.

Many people confuse pleasure with joy. Pleasure is a one-time thing while inner joy is a state of being. Living a carnal life will lead to eternal separation from God. God wants the best for you and sometimes the things we want are actually bad for us. Those worldly pleasures will not fill that void. Changing how you think is the start of this different path. God gives us all we need. When I was at my lowest, I figured out that no one was coming to save me, so I had to save myself. I had to work out my own salvation (Philippians 2:12-13). I moved forward knowing that God wanted more for me. God anchored and guided me through the process.

Ephesians 2:10 says, "We are God's masterpiece." Stop disagreeing with God because God loves us unconditionally and says that we are His workmanship. Next time, you look in the mirror, tell yourself, "I matter, because God loves me." Now that you know that you are good enough, change how you think so that the inside and the outside are in balance. We reap what we sow, and until we each see ourselves as God sees us, we will not become the people that He wants us to become.

"Who do you represent?"

Each day, we have a choice, we can serve the light and the Lord, or we can serve the darkness or the adversary (satan). Today, I wish to ask all of us the question, "who do we represent?"

2 Corinthians 5:20 states, "Now then, we are Ambassadors for Christ, as though God were pleading through us; we implore you on Christ's behalf, be reconciled to God.

I love this verse because it tells me that we, as Christians, are called to represent Christ on Earth by making Him the Lord of our life. All nations send representatives to foreign countries around the world. These nations establish embassies to carry out the national security directives of the country that sent them. The head of the embassy is an ambassador and he acts as the personal representative of the president of his/her country. The ambassadors and the representatives inside the embassy watch over the interest of their country. As born-again Christians, we now represent Christ. The verse of scripture above showed me that we must all reconcile the past with the present. Our job is to serve God and watch over His interest in this world.

The devil runs wild in this world, and darkness has become more prevalent than the light. Just look at the TV shows that are popular to include a new reality show called "Naked Dating". The world is not our friend. The desires of this age point to darkness and things which represent the devil. Too few Christians actually live a life which show that they live for Christ. The world is full of pretenders and most of those pretenders are searching for meaning to their life. People seek to be heard through blogging about their daily life. Reality TV shows have created a generation of voyeurs, people who rather watch the lives of others than experience life for themselves. I heard one Christian author, Nancy Moser, state that, "We should not cooperate with the world, but change it."

We must be the change we want to see in our households and neighborhoods, changing the world so it will be ready when Christ returns. We first must change ourselves and then move to change the world. As Christians, we are to be Christ-like. This word, Christian, means that you and I are followers of Christ. Now, before I choose to accept Christ as my personal savior, I would have told you that I was a Christian because I occasionally attended church. That said, I didn't have a close and intimate relationship with Christ. I was not a follower of Christ but just a fan. My religion didn't change me. I didn't represent Christ because I didn't allow Christ to enter my heart. Today, I am more informed because I have read the beautiful, wonderful words of God in the 66 love letters He wrote for us. Religion should change us so that we bring love into the universe instead of chaos. Today, I have love in my heart because of Christ.

Everywhere we go, we are representatives of Christ. Sometimes the only Jesus some people will see is us. We are His hands, feet, mouth and should always keep that fact at the forefronts of our hearts and minds. We hand out business cards each day but it should say "Embassy of the Kingdom of Heaven, Ambassador for Christ." The Bible states in Philippians 3:20-21, "For our citizenship is in heaven, from which we also eagerly wait for the savior, the Lord Jesus Christ, who will transform our lowly body that it may be conformed to His glorious body, according to the working by which He is able even to subdue all things to Himself." If our citizenship is in heaven then we should be working for the benefit of that kingdom and not this world.

"But seek first the kingdom of heaven and His righteousness, and all these things shall be added to you (Mathew 6:33)." I could just focus on this one verse because it gives us the roadmap on how we should live, a Christ-like framework. Putting God first as His ambassadors is my subject.

2 Corinthians 5:15 states, "and He died for all, that those who live should live no longer for themselves, but for Him who died for them

and rose again." Once a person makes Jesus the center of their lives, there is a change. "Therefore if anyone is in Christ, he is a new creation, old things have passed away, behold all things have become new (2 Corinthians 5:17). I ask myself, "if I am a Christian, where is the change? Do others see the change within me?"

Being an ambassador for Christ in spirit and truth will bring you joy. How does one become an Ambassador for Christ in spirit and truth? It starts with looking inside of ourselves with a Godly consciousness with shame or condemnation but in order to serve Him. "But let a man examine himself…(1 Corinthians 11:28)." This verse discusses that we should examine ourselves. The process starts here and we have been empowered by the creator for every good thing. Being an ambassador for Christ isn't easy in this world we live in. We can learn how to be representatives of Christ through a few simple steps.

Listen and be open to change. We must seek to hear that small still voice of God by creating an atmosphere to hear from God. The Bible tells us that God is faithful to those who follow Him. We should work to maintain a listening ear, always open to being directed my God. Proverbs 8:34 states, "Blessed (happy or fortunate) is the man who listens to Me, watching daily at my gates, waiting at the posts of my doors."

Surrender to a new way to doing things. Life as a Christian is still a struggle at times but Philippians 4:13 tells me that "I can do all things through Christ who strengthens me." This is a promise from God. I had to train myself to follow God without question. When I started reading the Bible, I learned that the things that pleased God was actually good for me. Today, I have faith in God that He would do what He promised even if I couldn't see things happening in the natural. Surrendering is about having steadfast faith.

We repent (turn away) from our old life and live differently. "Godly sorrow produces repentance (2 Corinthians 7:10)." I regret my former conduct when I lived for the world but there is no shame or condemnation in Christ but I use the past to motivate me for Christ. Don't let your past hinder you or hold you back, allow your past to motivate you. After I fell into depression, I was forced to look at myself and my actions because I caused my own pain. My pain allowed me to see things in a different light and challenge existing beliefs. My struggles saved me because I came to see that Jesus was all I needed to have a great life. I am thankful for my past and the struggles of the past because I learned more from those times than when I was doing well. The pain of the past freed me because I would have never sought a different way to live. Sometimes God has to allow us to fall so that we will look up, at Him. God had been seeking to get my attention for years but I ignored Him. Are you ignoring Him now?

How to be an effective ambassador for Christ? - We listen, are open to change, surrender and repent, and we start to live within the will of God. We start to seek to know the mind of God each day. We learn the mind of God through the reading of His word. The Bible contains light to direct our steps and provides daily spiritual food.

Once we are on a Godly path, we then seek to share what we have learned with others. We lead others to Christ by our actions and words as His ambassador. We don't have to be ministers or preachers but can be that Godly person on our job each day. We can live each day as Ambassadors of Christ through our thoughts, words and actions. One of the most important ways to be an ambassador for Christ is through our attitude each day, how we deal with and treat others is one of the most visible ways to show the world who we represent.

Peter 2:9 states, "You will be my witness..." Our personal testimony tells more than anything else. God has given us a message to share. "Those who believe in the Son of God have a testimony of God in them (1 John 5:10a)." Further, we learn in 1 Thessalonians 1:8, "You're the message." This is what being an ambassador for Christ is all about. Find the role you should play and use it to glorify God. Romans 8:28 states, "And we know that all things work together for good to those who love God, to those who are called according to His purpose."

Too many people let fear and doubts direct their steps. We must not let fear dictate our future. In Joshua 1:1-9, God tells Joshua three times to "Be strong and good courage" because the Lord knew that he would face certain hurdles in the world. Further, God stated in Joshua 1:8, "This Book of Law shall not depart from your mouth, but you shall meditate on it day and night, that you may observe to do according to all that is written in it. For them you will make your way prosperous, and then you will have good success." When we follow the ways of God, then we will be prosperous and can lead others to the truth. God promises in that section of Joshua that He would never leave nor forsake us. We must believe what God says and live a life pleasing to Him.

We should want to do what is said in Ephesians 4:22 when we are told 'to put off our former conduct'. Later in Ephesians 5:2, we are told to "Walk in love." A few verses later we are told to "Walk as Children of light." Being an ambassador for Christ must be a goal for every believer each day. When we lived for the world, we were in darkness. But now, we have heard the truth and read the truth, we must live differently. The battle for good and evil is being fought all over the world. Question: where are you in this battle? Are you an agent of chaos or an agent of God?

Each day, the battle for the world takes place in our hearts, souls and minds. We must eradicate the sinful patterns in our lives. I am preaching to myself too because I still have challenges. I still get angry, judge and have unloving feelings but the difference today for me is that I understand my battle and my enemy. I ask myself each day, "if I say I love God, how can I do what God hates?" I ask myself this question so I can be better. I ask myself, "Am I moving closer to God each day?"

God wants us to honor Him each day through our actions. When we honor God, joy is the natural result. This is how we can become upright ambassadors of Christ each day. We are all spiritual beings and we must feed the spirit each day or our spirit will start to decay.

There are many people out here who are depressed and without hope but Christ came and died so that love and hope will flow in and through us to others. We are beings of hope and love but the world tries to corrupt our essential nature, our Godly nature. We must continue to fight the good fight of faith each day so that we can represent the Lord in the world. In the world today, where are you in this on-going battle between the people of God and the people of evil? Our goal each day should be to act as the hands and feet of Christ.

Jesus tells us in Mathew 5:16, "Let your light shine so before men, that they may see your good works and glorify your father in heaven."

John 10:10 tells us that Jesus came so that we may have life and have it more abundantly! God gave us all we would ever need in His son, Jesus Christ. Shouldn't we give the Lord our very best each day? I leave you with a verse from the Apostle Paul to the church at

Philippi, "Only let your conduct be worthy of the gospel of Christ...(Philippians 1:27)."

If you do what you can do for Christ, God will do what you can't! **We have the DNA of the almighty God running through our veins. We were created by God and are of God according to 1 John 4:4**.

I challenge all of us to strive each day to be the men and women whom God created us to be, living up to our potential so we can glorify God in all we do or say.

"These things I have spoken to you that my joy might be in you, so that your joy might be full."

Jesus (John 15:11)

Did you ever run across the old children's book called Mr. Happy? His story goes like this: One day he leaves his very happy home and goes walking in the neighborhood. He finds a door and wonders to himself, "Who lives here?" When he goes through the door he is led down a long staircase and into the room where Mr. Miserable lives. Mr. Happy leads Mr. Miserable out of the room, up the stairs and back to his home, where Mr. Miserable stays for some time. Over the time he is there, Mr. Happy begins to rub off on him and one day Mr. Miserable finds himself beginning to do something he has never done before. He smiles. The story ends with the lesson that if we're ever miserable, we can fix it by smiling!

I believe it's possible for some people to help themselves just by turning their frown upside down. A simple thing such as controlling your facial expression can change your life for the better. For example - smiling is thought to be good for our health. Researchers are finding that wearing a smile brings certain benefits, like slowing down the heart and reducing stress. The act of smiling can make you feel happier. I always keep a smile on my face because I have the joy of the Lord in my heart. Some research have suggested that only a full and genuine smile affects the body in positive ways. I would put a smile on my face in the morning and would immediately feel better. I started smiling when I worked out in the gym and feel better there also. I am now a firm believer that anyone can affect their mental health in a positive or negative by what they do with their face.

Smiling became a conscious decision each day for me. I would start praying and then smiling and then I would feel better. I started to think better thoughts when I smiled also. A study published in the journal Psychological Science in November 2012 found that people who smiled after engaging in stress-inducing tasks showed a greater reduction in heart rate than people who maintained a neutral facial expression. I suggest that when the face smile the body starts to react as if there is something to be happy about so the body relaxes. Now I also believe the same about people who frown all the time, increased stress level and increased heart rate. It's the same with thoughts, when we have evil or negative thoughts, our body responds in a negative fashion and there is a reaction based on those thoughts. Being more mindful in every way can help give us the life we all want, a life of purpose and meaning with inner peace and true contentment.

I love using the example of smiling because it was a practice I used to fight against the conditioning of the past. Today, I love to smile and it always make me feel better and it's an outward testimony for me about the goodness of God. You can always control your attitude each day. It was also a characteristic of the divine grace which resulted in an attitude of cheerfulness, calm delight and great gladness based on living a life in the Spirit. My joy was a result of my faith in God and was not affected by the circumstances of life.

My joy comes from salvation, from an awareness of God's power to act on my behalf, and from the blessings of a daily walk with God. It's through His word, prayer and meditation that I was able to get close to God. Some theologians say that there is a strong bond between suffering and joy for the Christian. The joy for the Lord allowed me to transform my life. I had faith that joy would always come in the morning. I also smiled because I had peace, the peace which the Holy Spirit gave me. The peace of God is an inner peace which replaces anger, guilt, and worry. I had been seeking that all my life and tried to fill me life with all of those exterior things hoping it would give me peace. The Bible asks us to do our best to live at peace with everyone, to seek peace and pursue it. Peace with our fellows allow us to help fulfill Jesus' thoughts regarding being a peacemaker. If our thoughts are peace-like then we can be a peacemaker but if our thoughts are chaotic and based on the whims of life then there will be no balance.

Some of us can be moody. We are stressed out and confused about our lives and the lives of people we live with. We deal with real depression, real anxiety, and real mood disorders. Many of us chronically feel like we're running just to keep up. So how do messages about joy work for real people like us, whose lives are a little more complicated than Mr. Happy? How do we do this thing called reality without it looking like a Hallmark card? How does joy mesh with stress and broken dreams and broken relationships and the death of people we love and the kind of anxiety and depression that goes deeper than a bad mood or a bad day?

If Jesus said, "I came that you might have joy, and that you might have it to the full," then how do I acquire that inheritance. Here's what I believe: I believe biblical joy is not only attainable, but is the normal state of the Spirit-filled life. Christians are meant to grow in joy. And as we've already said, maybe your temperament or approach to life or other circumstances makes this more of a challenge for you. But as a follower of Jesus, filled with the Holy Spirit, it is your inheritance. And there are things we can do to clear the channel so we have the most opportunity to experience the fruit of the Spirit-filled life.

Let's start with a definition. What is biblical joy?

1. Joy is a spiritually generated response to God's goodness.

2. Joy is a deep, down assurance that the quality of my life is not rooted in my feelings or circumstances but in the love, cover and hope of a good and faithful God. Spiritual joy comes from a deeper place than our everyday emotions, which are also gifts from God. The difference is that emotions don't have roots, but spiritual fruit does.

4. Joy is a natural fruit of the Spirit-filled life

.

What are the habits of these Spirit-filled people? I count at least seven:

1. Joyful people forgive easily.
2. Joyful people have learned the value of intimacy.
3. Joyful people have mastered the discipline of waiting.

4. Joyful people are gratefully generous.
5. Joyful people focus on progress not perfection.
6. Joyful people maintain a mood rooted in something bigger than themselves.
7. Joyful people pursue the Holy Spirit.

The Greek word used in the New Testament is Chairo.

Chairo means "favorably disposed, leaning towards" and it's a synonym of the word (grace") in the sense of "to delight in God's grace" ("rejoice") – literally, to experience God's grace (favor), be conscious (glad) for His grace.

Chairo can also be defined to rejoice, be glad, to rejoice exceedingly, to be well, thrive, and to be cheerful or calmly happy. The New Testament mentions 'Chairo' 68 times.

"Rejoice in the Lord always. Again I will say, rejoice!" Philippians 4:4

"Not that I speak in regard to need, for I have learned in whatever state I am, to be content:" Philippians 4:11

Did you know that the Apostle Paul was in a Roman prison when he wrote the book of Ephesians, Philippians, Colossians and Philemon which is why they are called the Prison epistles?

Paul legitimately feared that he might be put to death. And yet, rather than focusing on the negative aspects of his death, he focused on the positive outcome his death might bring. He was optimistic, and as a result, he was able to rejoice. Paul did not feel only joy, but he did feel true joy. And this joy provided him with a desire to press onward, and it gave purpose to his suffering.

Romans 12:12 states "Be joyful in hope, patient in affliction, faithful in prayer."

Your mess is part of the process, to progress in sanctification. We grow and mature as believers as we read the word of God and trust the Lord. "being confident of this, that he who began a good work in you will carry it on to completion until the day of Christ Jesus (Philippians 1:6)." Are you living with this confidence?

2 Corinthians 3:18 state, "And we all, who with unveiled faces contemplate the Lord's glory, are being transformed into his image with ever-increasing glory, which comes from the Lord, who is the Spirit."

Let's examine the Parable of the Sower in Matthew 13:3-9

"Then He spoke many things to them in parables, saying: "Behold, a sower went out to sow. And as he sowed, some seed fell by the wayside; and the birds came and devoured them. Some fell on stony places, where they did not have much earth; and they immediately sprang up because they had no depth of earth. But when the sun was up they were scorched, and because they had no root they withered away. And some fell among thorns, and the thorns sprang up and choked them. But others fell on good ground and yielded a crop:

some a hundredfold, some sixty, some thirty. He who has ears to hear, let him hear!"

Some seed fell on the:
- Wayside; these got devoured by the birds. Some Christians haven't hidden God's word deep into their heart. Have you ever lived on the wayside? The word of God will center you and bring you joy.
- Stony places; these got scorched because it didn't have a root. Some Christians still have stony places in their hearts which prevent joy from being nurtured.
- Thorns; these got choked out by the very things it fell into. Have you ever fell into something that you knew weren't good for you? That seed mentioned in the above parable can also be thought of the seed of joy! We must make good decisions in our life.

Our mess doesn't have to define us and it can allow others to see the glory of God through our transformation.

Challenge your assumptions! I believe "joy is your birth right as a Christian. Joy is yours but you just have to believe that it true."

Let's check out another scripture in Nehemiah, **"So Ezra the priest brought the Law before the assembly of men and women and all who could hear with understanding on the first day of the seventh month. Then he read from it in the open square that was in front of the Water Gate from morning until midday, before the men and women and those who could understand; and the ears of all the people were attentive to the Book of the Law (Nehemiah 8:2-3)."**

"And Ezra blessed the LORD, the great God. Then all the people answered, "Amen, Amen!" while lifting up their hands. And they bowed their heads and worshiped the LORD with their faces to the ground (Nehemiah 8:6)."

"And Nehemiah, who was the governor, Ezra the priest and scribe, and the Levites who taught the people said to all the people, "This day is holy to the LORD your God; do not mourn nor weep." For all the people wept, when they heard the words of the Law. Then he said to them, "Go your way, eat the fat, drink the sweet, and send portions to those for whom nothing is

prepared; for this day is holy to our Lord. Do not sorrow, <u>for the joy of the LORD is your strength</u>." So the Levites quieted all the people, saying, "Be still, for the day is holy; do not be grieved." And all the people went their way to eat and drink, to send portions and rejoice greatly, because they understood the words that were declared to them (Nehemiah 8:9-12)."

--The early church was characterized by gladness and the joy of the Lord (Acts 2:46; 13:52), and "joy in the Holy Spirit" is a distinguishing mark of the kingdom of God (Romans 14:17).

--Joy is part of the fruit of the Spirit (Galatians 5:22). In fact, it is our Christian duty to rejoice in the Lord (Philippians 3:1; 4:4; 1 Thessalonians 5:16). In Christ, the believer is "filled with an inexpressible and glorious joy" (1 Peter 1:8).

Because of its supernatural origin, the joy of the Lord—our gladness of heart—is present even through the trials of life. We know we are children of God, and no one can snatch us away from Him (John 10:28–29).

We are heirs to "an inheritance that can never perish, spoil or fade," and no one can steal it from us (1 Peter 1:4; Matthew 6:20). We see the Author and Finisher of our faith, and, we know who wins in the end (Hebrews 12:2; Psalm 2).

"Restore unto me the joy of thy salvation; and uphold me with thy free spirit (Psalm 51:12)."

As a man thinks in his heart, so is he (Proverbs 23:7). You have to believe that joy is your birthright as a Christian. It's already inside. You just have to nurture it through having a made-up mind and allowing the Holy Spirit to do the work inside.

We do our part and let the Lord do His part. Our part:

Prayer

Read the bible!

Meditation on God's word!

Selfless service to others to Glorify God!

Study to show ourselves approved (bible and other Godly books)!

Stay teachable and Look for the lesson!

Confess your sin to the Lord and seek, long for and lean on the Holy Spirit to encourage, empower and deliver you!

Maintain a Godly attitude understanding that God wants us to be joyful!

"Jesus said "Until now you have asked nothing in My name. Ask, and you will receive, that your joy may be full." John 16:24

"These things I have spoken to you, that in Me you may have peace. In the world you will have tribulation; but be of good cheer, I have overcome the world." John 16:33

Peace and joy are connected! If you are in a tumultuous living situation then it will be more difficult to have true inner joy.

So many times in life we tell ourselves lies. We may believe that these lies help us because there are times when it can be so painful to tell ourselves the truth that we will do everything possible to avoid it. It can be very difficult to handle the truth. Sometimes in the natural truth can break us but in for those of us in Christ, the truth sets us free. I hope this book sets some people free.

The Greek word used in the New Testament is "Chairo." I think it's important to know what the original word from the Bible says because it makes the word come alive.

Chairo means "favorably disposed, leaning towards" and it's a synonym of the word (grace") in the sense of "to delight in God's grace" ("rejoice") – literally, to experience God's grace (favor), be conscious (glad) for His grace.

You see how this expands what we know as Joy or contentment.

Chairo can be defined also as ("glad or joyful for God's grace"). I could stop right there and teach from that but I will go on because if your heart is receptive and your mind is alert, I think that you will get a blessing.

68 times 'Chairo' is used in the New Testament so that means that it is an important Christian concept.

So, I want to start out with the Apostle Paul with the 4th chapter of Philippians. This is an important text for the joy-filled Christian. I'll start with 2 specific verses from Philippians 4.

""Rejoice in the Lord always. Again I will say, rejoice (Philippians 4:4)."

"Not that I speak in regard to need, for I have learned in whatever state I am, to be content (Philippians 4:11)."

The Apostle Paul was in a Roman prison when he wrote the book of Ephesians, Philippians, Colossians and Philemon which is why they are called the Prison epistles.

Philippians is a beautiful letter Paul wrote to a church he loved. The church in Philippi was established by Paul and Silas on Paul's second missionary journey (Acts 16:11-40). Lydia and her household, and the jailor and his household, were among the first converts. Philippians was written to thank the church for the gift they sent to help Paul while he was in prison (Philippians 4:10-20).

Even though Paul was a prisoner when he wrote to Philippi, he is full of joy. The key word in Philippians is "joy."

This word, and other forms of it such as "rejoice," is found at least fifteen times in the four chapters of this epistle. Philippians teaches us that Christians can be happy even if we are in the midst of hardship and suffering. We are joyful because of the hope we have in Christ.

This concept of Joy is a great help in Christian perseverance. Life can be a challenge for people especially those who don't have the same mindset of Christ (Paul speaks of us having the same mindset as Christ in Philippians 2:5.)

I love the Apostle Paul because Paul himself concentrated on finding joy in order to persevere through his distressing circumstances. And by his example, he encouraged the believers in Philippi to do so as well. For instance, in Philippians 1:18-20, Paul spoke of his joy in this way:

In chapter 1 of Philippians, Paul says, "I will continue to rejoice, for I know that through your prayers and the help given by the Spirit of Jesus Christ, what has happened to me will turn out for my deliverance. I eagerly expect and hope that ... Christ will be exalted in my body, whether by life or by death (Philippians 1:18-20)."

Paul legitimately feared that he might be put to death. And yet, rather than focusing on the negative aspects of his death, he focused on the positive outcome his death might bring. He was optimistic, and as a result, he was able to rejoice.

Notice that in this case Paul's joy was not a naive denial of pain and suffering, or even an overwhelming emotion of happiness. On the contrary, as we have seen, there was much sadness and suffering mixed into Paul's feelings as well. But despite his troubles, Paul truly was able to look at the good things in life and to rejoice over them. He could think about honoring Christ through a courageous death and be satisfied — even pleased — at Christ's exaltation. And that satisfaction and pleasure constituted joy. Paul did not feel only joy, but he did feel true joy. And this joy provided him with a desire to press onward, and it gave purpose to his suffering.

Don't waste your pain. Use it to help someone else. Your past pain is important because it allows you to understand others in pain and demonstrate how your past doesn't define you. It becomes a testimony for the glory of God.

The book of Philippians has many rich and wonderful truths to teach us about standing firm in our Christian faith, and about living righteously before our holy God, even during times of suffering and distress. As we submit ourselves to these teachings, we will realize how utterly important perseverance is, and we will be greatly encouraged to dedicate ourselves to this awesome task. And most importantly, as we succeed in our own perseverance by following Paul's advice, and as we help others to persevere as well, we will bring glory and honor to our exalted Lord Jesus Christ.

Paul encouraged the Philippians to be joyful because the Lord was near, whether as their help in time of need, or as the king who would return to bring his reign of peace to all the earth. In either case, joy would motivate and enable the Philippians to fend off anxiety. And therefore, it would prepare them to persevere until the Lord's return.

By patterning our mindset after Paul's, by focusing on humility and optimism and joy, we can strengthen ourselves against anxiety and despair. It is inevitable that hardship will come and that we will suffer — sometimes greatly. So, when we do, we need to remember Paul's example and advice. We need to temper our suffering with a humble spirit, and to remain hopeful by thinking about the many good things we have in this life and the next. And we need to overcome the troubles of our condition by making a conscious decision to rejoice over those things in our lives that are still worthy of joy. In these ways, we can be strengthened, with God's help, to persevere.

Christians must understand that no matter what they are going through they still needed to rejoice in the fact that Jesus Christ is our strong tower and that they must remain joyful, cheerful and calmly happy through it all.

The Greek word can also mean "to be cheerful, or calmly happy." It's all about Christ, not about our feelings. This world is not our home. In other words this one Greek word "Chairo" can be used to describe a behavior and attitude. Joy gives us power because it's about focusing on the wonderful promises of God instead of our circumstances.

Romans 12:12 states "Be joyful in hope, patient in affliction, faithful in prayer."

Love, joy, peace are the 1st three "fruit of the Spirit". There is a reason that it's in this order because Love is the greatest commandment from God and when we truly love with all our heart, soul, mind and strength—the result is joy and followed by and in conjunction with peace.

Love, joy and peace puts us in harmony with God and with others. The more I study the bible and my life as I dedicate it to the Lord as my reasonable service. I understand an even greater need for Jesus. As we get closer to the image of God, we understand our even greater need for Christ.

If love, joy and peace is in harmony with the Lord then perhaps hatred, anger and chaos is at war with God or disharmony with God.

You can live in victory! There are just too many bitter Christians, too many Christian seeking retribution not peace. In Deuteronomy, God tells us to "Choose life!" Choosing Life is "choosing love, joy and peace."

Juanita Bynum has a song called "I don't mind waiting" where she says, "If you knew my story then you would know my praise." The joy-filled Christian understands that praise is a vital part of living in joy. Chairo is connected to praise and gratitude. I know I have reason to praise the Lord because the devil put the gun in my hand but Jesus said not today.

The devil can't do anything he wants. "The Earth is the Lords, and everything in it, the world, and all who live in it (Psalm 24:1)."

Stop giving the devil the power. Lucifer, the fallen angel, now known as satan or the devil is a created being by the Lord like us. The devil can't make you do it. I often say that out of our mess, God gives us a message.

Your mess is part of the process, to progress in sanctification.

Remember the Good Samaritan in Luke 10:30 states, "Then Jesus answered and said: "A certain man went down from Jerusalem to Jericho, and fell among thieves, who stripped him of his clothing, wounded him, and departed, leaving him half dead." He fell among thieves...The robbers stripped him, beat him and went away leaving him half dead. See there are some Christians out here who are half dead. These Christians are not living in victory, living a life of joy-filled hope each day.

"This is why it is said: "Wake up, sleeper, rise from the dead, and Christ will shine on you."" (Ephesians 5:14)." This book is about joy or contentment. I believe that Christians should be the most joy-filled people on this planet. Can I get an amen?

Christians should have hope, not like those who don't have a close personal relationship with Jesus. Christians should be "bout that life!" That abundant life, that "life" that Jesus came to give us. The Holy Spirit empowers us to be more than we could ever be in the natural.

Only God can turn a mess into a message. And we all have a mess (if we didn't then we would be perfect and wouldn't need Jesus). Don't allow your mess to become other's mess. Own your mess and then give it to Jesus; and watch what happened when you fully surrender. Not by might, nor by power but by the Holy Spirit. Our mess doesn't have to define us and it can allow others to see the glory of God through our transformation. Challenge your assumptions and believe that joy is your birthright as a believer! Believe that "joy is your birth right as a Christian." Joy is yours but you just have to believe that it true."

Some Christians will read this and already start all the reasons in their mind why they can't do it. What do you have to lose?

Your bitterness, anger, pain etc. That's what you have to loose!

The joy of the Lord is your strength. Is it? Or are these just words? This is a promise from God!

Joy is my birth right as a born again Holy Ghost filled believer in the redeeming and atoning work of Jesus Christ of the cross. All we have to do is believe.

Hebrews 11:6 says, "But without faith it is impossible to [walk with God and] please Him, for whoever comes [near] to God must [necessarily] believe that God exists and that He rewards those who [earnestly and diligently] seek Him."

Nehemiah provides great insight in the concept of joy. **"For the joy of the Lord is your strength (Nehemiah 8:10)" is the central verse in this passage in Nehemiah.**

--Nehemiah told the repentant Israelites that the joy of the Lord would be their strength (Nehemiah 8:10).

The early church was characterized by gladness and the joy of the Lord (Acts 2:46; 13:52), and "joy in the Holy Spirit" is a distinguishing mark of the kingdom of God (Romans 14:17). Those who are part of the kingdom share in the kingdom's delight.

Joy is part of the fruit of the Spirit (Galatians 5:22). In fact, it is our Christian duty to rejoice in the Lord (Philippians 3:1; 4:4; 1 Thessalonians 5:16). In Christ, the believer is "filled with an inexpressible and glorious joy" (1 Peter 1:8).

Because of its supernatural origin, the joy of the Lord—our gladness of heart—is present even through the trials of life. We know we are children of God, and no one can snatch us away from Him (John 10:28–29).

We are heirs to "an inheritance that can never perish, spoil or fade," and no one can steal it from us (1 Peter 1:4; Matthew 6:20). We see the Author and Finisher of our faith, and, we know who wins in the end (Hebrews 12:2; Psalm 2).

Faith is the victory that overcomes the world, and the joy of the Lord is our strength. Adverse circumstances, instead of hindering our faith, can actually enhance our joy.

Paul and Silas knew adversity as they sat with their feet in the stocks in a Philippian jail cell. Their legal rights had been violated. They had been arrested without cause and beaten without a trial. At midnight, since they couldn't sleep, they sang—loudly—the praises of the Lord they were serving (Acts 16:25). A miracle soon followed (verse 26).

The apostles in Jerusalem were arrested—twice—and ordered not to preach in Jesus' name. The second time they faced the court, they were beaten. Unfazed, they returned home "rejoicing because they had been counted worthy of suffering disgrace for the Name" and ready to preach some more (Acts 5:41). Of course, the apostles were only following the example of our Lord, who had "for the joy set before him . . . endured the cross, scorning its shame" (Hebrews 12:2).

The joy of the Lord may be inexplicable to the one who does not possess it.

But, for the believer in Christ, the joy of the Lord comes as naturally as grapes on a vine. As we abide in Christ, the True Vine, we the branches are full of His strength and vitality, and the fruit we produce, including joy, is His doing (John 15:5).

Sometimes I think Christians can be like babies, they want to be approved, coddled, catered to and entertained. When will people truly grow up so they know, believe and internalize that Jesus is enough!

Is Jesus enough? Today, tomorrow, next week or will you let the world steal your joy. Joy is found in Jesus Christ. Joy is found in running your race. There are people in this world who only bring chaos. Lord is the gladness of heart that comes from knowing God, abiding in Christ, and being filled with the Holy Spirit.

When Jesus was born, the angels announced "good tidings of great joy" (Luke 2:10).

All who find Jesus know, with the shepherds of the nativity, the joy He brings. Even before His birth, Jesus had brought joy, as attested to in Mary's song (Luke 1:47) and by John's response to hearing Mary's voice as he "leaped for joy" in his mother's womb (Luke 1:44).

Jesus exemplified joy in His ministry. He was no glum ascetic; rather, His enemies accused Him of being too joyful on occasion (Luke 7:34).

Jesus described Himself as bridegroom enjoying a wedding feast (Mark 2:18–20);

He "rejoiced in the Holy Spirit" (Luke 10:21);

He spoke of "my joy" (John 15:11) and promised to give His disciples a lifetime supply of it (John 16:24).

Joy is reflected in many of Jesus' parables, including the three stories in Luke 15, which mention "rejoicing in the presence of the angels" (Luke 15:10) and end with a joyful shepherd, a joyful woman, and a joyful father.

Jesus said Matthew 7:26, "You can identify them by their fruit, that is, by the way they act. Can you pick grapes from thorn bushes, or figs from thistles?" Jesus didn't say that you will recognize them from their words.

See the Pharisees loved long speeches and beautiful words but they had no fruit. The teachers of the law forgot the most important point from Deuteronomy which said you will love the Lord with all your heart soul mind and strength.

Jesus said "By this My Father is glorified, that you bear much fruit; so you will be My disciples. (John 15:8)."

This book can encourage, empower and deliver some who hear this message but for the pretenders they will get nothing as the seed of God's word will fall by the way side.

We all need to stand firm and be on the offensive against the forces of evil in this world.

Say out loud "Devil, get behind me you ain't gonna steal my joy." Perhaps that devil is a person in your circle who always bring trouble. Don't let anyone steal your seed like in the parable of the sower. Make your mind up to live in joyful expectation each day and keep it set.

"We are God's handiwork, created in Christ Jesus to do good works (Ephesians 2:10)."

And we must always reflect on our lives to make sure that we are moving towards the upward calling each day. The bible makes clear that we must assess our own actions.

--"Let each one examine themselves…1 Corinthians 11:28."
--Galatians 6:4 states, "Each one should test their own actions. Then they can take pride in themselves alone, without comparing themselves to someone else."
--2 Corinthians 13:5 says, "Examine yourselves to see whether you are in the faith; test yourselves. Do you not realize that Christ Jesus is in you--unless, of course, you fail the test?"

Feed your faith, not your fear!

Doubt your fear and believe in your promises of God each day!

Acknowledge your fears before God.

Fear will keep you from living in abundant joy.

Fear will strip, trip and grip you so that you can't be who God created you to be.

I'm not afraid of death. Because to die is to gain. Absent in the body is to be present with the lord. The enemy in me, did his best to take me out, what can man do to me. See I'm a minister of the good news of Jesus Christ and I know who I am in Christ. I'm not concerned if you don't like me but I am concerned about your relationship with Jesus and about you growing and maturing in Christ.

"Having a good attitude doesn't always mean that you feel like it. You just know deep down that the Word of God is true!" Joyce Meyer

"Restore unto me the joy of thy salvation; and uphold me with thy free spirit." Psalm 51:12

You have to believe that Joy is your birthright as a Christian. It's already inside.

You just have to nurture it through having a made-up mind and allowing the Holy Spirit to do the work inside:

The Bible says that you are a "new creation" (2 Corinthians 5:17) when you decide to follow Christ. Your old "self" is gone, and the new is here. As a result, we want to help you grow in your faith and in your knowledge of Jesus.

Habits to live by for the joy-filled Christian

Read the Bible Daily

The Bible is God's inspired instruction manual for us. It has many answers to help you live a life that pleases God. A good place to start is in the New Testament with the Gospel of Luke. The book of Acts is a great follow up; it contains the exciting story of how Christ's disciples spread the Good News about His death, burial and resurrection.

As you read, ask God to give you understanding and wisdom: Open my eyes to see the wonderful truths in your law (Psalm 119:18). Think about what you read: study and analyze it. Write down questions you have and ask a mature Christian to help clarify your understanding.

Pray with God Daily

Talk with God often. Talk over your problems with Him. Thank Him for who He is and what He has done for you. Confess your sins to

Him and admit your weaknesses. Ask God to help show you how to live a life that pleases Him. Pray for others, that they too may choose to follow Jesus Christ as their Savior and give Him the leadership of their lives.

Depend on the Holy Spirit

The Bible teaches that now that you have chosen to follow Christ, the Holy Spirit actually lives within you (Romans 5:5; John 14:16-17). The Holy Spirit will teach you, guide you, and strengthen you in times of need.

Attend Church Regularly

When you became a Christian, you began an authentic personal relationship with Jesus. However, it is important to also have authentic connections with other Christians. In a fireplace, many logs burn together creating heat and warmth, but a log by itself quickly dies out. Likewise, we too need the fellowship of other believers to keep our faith vibrant and growing. The Church is a place where you can worship God and make Him the focus of your life.

Be of Service to Others

Jesus tells us repeatedly to give our lives to serve Him, and to serve others. If you try to keep your life for yourself, you will lose it. But if you give up your life for my sake and for the sake of the Good News, you will find true life (Mark 8:35). The more you give yourself in service to others, the more you will enjoy your Christian life.

Conquer Your Doubts

At times you may doubt that you really are a Christian. Perhaps you have failed or surrendered repeatedly to temptation. Remember, you were not saved because of how good of a person you are, but by putting your trust in what Christ has already done for you. Trust the truth found in God's Word over your own subjective feelings. I write this to you who believe in the Son of God, so that you may know that you have eternal life (I John 5:13).

Live One Day at a Time

Too often we become anxious about what might happen tomorrow. The Bible promises that God will meet our needs, if only we will seek first His righteousness (see Matthew 6:33-34). God's grace will be sufficient to meet the challenges that each new day brings.

Learn How to Deal with Temptation

Temptation is a part of life. It was an issue before you became a Christian, it still will be. You do not, however, have to yield to temptation to sin. The Bible says, God is faithful. He will keep the temptation from becoming so strong that you can't stand up against it. When you are tempted, He will show you a way out so that you will not give in to it (1 Corinthians 10:13).

Be prepared to take advantage of God's "way out" of temptation, whether it means that you "flee" the scene of temptation (I Timothy 6:11), or that you stay on the scene and "resist" it (James 4:7; I Peter 5:8-9).

Tell Others about Jesus

Sharing with others about your new life in Jesus--by word or by action--can be one of the most satisfying and exciting experiences you have ever had. The Bible encourages us to always be prepared to give an answer to everyone who asks you to give the reason for the hope that you have (I Peter 3:15).

God has built us so that we would be joy-filled Christian. You are already built that way! Jesus left us his peace so then why are so many Christians living without peace.

So many people get in their own way. Jesus stated….John 14:12 states, "Very truly I tell you, whoever believes in me will do the works I have been doing, and they will do even greater things than these, because I am going to the Father."

You must not be persuaded otherwise for joy comes in the morning and because the Son of God loves you! Set your mind on joy and keep it set. We all need to have a made up mind, not being conformed but being transformed. Transformation isn't about

IMPROVING. It's about the indwelling Spirit completely regenerating our hearts and our minds to that of Christ.

Water conforms to a container but if you heat it to boiling point then the water is transformed into steam. The properties are changed. Are you transformed or just living the conformed life? Transformation into a new creature. What does transformation mean? It's a thorough or dramatic change in form or appearance. So if you see someone year after year with the same old mess, one has to ask where their fruit is.

Jesus said "By this My Father is glorified, that you bear much fruit; so you will be My disciples (John 15:8)."

You have greatness within you!

"You are of God, little children, and have overcome them, because He who is in you is greater than he who is in the world (I John 4:4)."

Choose to be an uncommon person!

Choose to be a peculiar believer, set apart to do good works!

The kingdom of heaven is within you! "For indeed, the kingdom of God is within you (Luke 17:21)."

Has Jesus brought you joy? If you have no joy then ask the Holy Spirit to bring you that joy and peace that surpasses all understanding. See peace is connected to joy. If you have no peace then you will have no joy. If you are stuck in a rut and are not fulfilling your God ordained purpose then I suggest you lean on, call on, and partner with the Holy Spirit to get more peace in your heart with will bring more joy.

There is greatness in you because the Kingdom of God is within you because God has given you His breath of life when He made you. Because you are made in the image of God who is perfect.

"Why do you think the Bible says "be perfect (Matthew 5:48)", or "be holy because I am holy (1 Peter 1:16)" if it was not possible?

Believers must know who they are in Christ. You are not this flesh, you are a new creature who has been transformed. That's how God sees you but how do you see yourself?

Too many Christians talk more about their problems and issues than they speak about their God and you see it on their countenance (their demeanor and attitude).

You can choose your attitude each day.

My joy comes from the Lord, and no matter what anyone says. This is the attitude all believers must have each day. Tell yourself this each morning! You must not be shaken.

You are blessed and highly favored!

Jesus came to set the captives free and came to give us life, and life more abundantly!

The Apostle Paul offers so much encouragement for the believer in Philippians. Paul wrote in unusual circumstances. He was in no quiet study dictating to some secretary, but in prison where the prospect was either execution or release. Yet he was a cheerful prisoner. He had no worries for himself. If he was to be put to death, then he would be with Christ. If he was to be released, then he would be free to continue his evangelical work with the church of Philippi. He tells us all this, and more, at the beginning of his letter (1:19-24). He forgets what lies behind and strains forward to what lies ahead, the heavenly call of God in Jesus Christ (3:13-14). Meanwhile, as he writes at the end of the letter, whether he had plenty or was in need, whether well-fed or going hungry, he was content (4:11-12). Paul learned how to be content and we must also learn how to be content.

Paul also found joy in his hope for future deliverance, which he described in verses 18b-21. He focused on the possibility that he might eventually be released from prison. But as we have said, during this time, Paul's suffering was so severe that even death would have been a welcomed relief. And so, he was encouraged by the hope that his suffering would be relieved, whether by his acquittal or by his death. He described his perspective in Philippians 1:18-21:

"Yes, and I will continue to rejoice, for I know that ... what has happened to me will turn out for my deliverance... whether by life or by death. For to me, to live is Christ and to die is gain (Philippians 1:18-21)."

And lastly, Paul exhorted the Philippians not to allow individual hardship to hinder their perseverance. He encouraged them to adopt a joyful perspective, and not to allow anxiety to discourage them. His thoughts are represented well by these words from Philippians 4:4-7:

"Rejoice in the Lord always. I will say it again: Rejoice! ... Do not be anxious about anything, but ... present your requests to God. And the peace of God ... will guard your hearts and your minds in Christ Jesus (Philippians 4:4-7)." Paul's practical instruction was that believers should ask God to relieve their anxieties. In some cases, God might do this by eliminating the troubling circumstances. But it would appear that in most cases, Paul expected the change to be one of heart and mind, of attitude and perspective.

The epistle to the Philippians can be applied to our lives in many different ways. Paul focused on encouraging others as he faced what might have been his last days on earth. From this perspective, one theme comes to the foreground: Paul's encouragement to the Philippians to persevere — to continue walking faithfully before God.

In Philippians, Paul's teachings on perseverance are most easily understood in terms of three main factors: the definition of perseverance; the necessity of perseverance; and the assurance of perseverance. Paul conceived of perseverance in terms of the dual ideas of true faith and righteous living. On the one hand, perseverance is maintaining our faith in the gospel of Christ, relying on his merit alone for our righteous standing before God. Paul wrote of this in Philippians 1:27, where he expressed his hope for the Philippians with these words:

"Stand firm in one spirit, contending as one man for the faith of the gospel (Philippians 1:27)."

As believers, we must remain steadfast in our commitment to the Gospel, never giving up our beliefs. This is what we mean when we speak of persevering in faith.

True faith in the gospel of Christ can be described in many ways, but listen to one central focus of Christian faith as Paul described it in Philippians 3:8-9:

Those whose faith is true possess the Holy Spirit, who works in them to guarantee their perseverance. Paul explains it simply in Philippians 1:6:

"[I am] confident of this, that he who began a good work in you will carry it on to completion until the day of Christ Jesus (Philippians 1:6)."

Paul gives us more encouragement in the following verses:

"Continue to work out your salvation with fear and trembling, for it is God who works in you to will and to act according to his good purpose (Philippians 2:12-13)."

The fear we are to have is not the fear that we might fall from grace, but overwhelming awe at the realization that God Almighty is working within each of us to ensure that we think and do what he wants. He controls our hearts and minds for his good purpose, which includes our perseverance so that there is no way we can fail to stand firm until the end.

By patterning our mindset after Paul's, by focusing on humility and optimism and joy, we can strengthen ourselves against anxiety and despair. It is inevitable that hardship will come and that we will suffer — sometimes greatly. So, when we do, we need to remember Paul's example and advice. We need to temper our suffering with a humble spirit, and to remain hopeful by thinking about the many good things we have in this life and the next. And we need to overcome the troubles of our condition by making a conscious decision to rejoice over those things in our lives that are still worthy of joy. In these ways, we can be strengthened, with God's help, to persevere.

In Philippians 4:7, Paul writes about God's the promise of peace, "And the peace of God, which surpasses all understanding, will guard your hearts and minds through Christ Jesus." This is an amazing promise!

Let go of your old self

"I have been crucified with Christ and I no longer live, but Christ lives in me. The life I now live in the body, I live by faith in the Son of God, who loved me and gave himself for me. Galatians 2:20

"Not that I have already attained, or am already perfected; but I press on, that I may lay hold of that for which Christ Jesus has also laid hold of me. Brethren, I do not count myself to have apprehended; but one thing I do, forgetting those things which are behind and reaching forward to those things which are ahead, I press toward the goal for the prize of the upward call of God in Christ Jesus. Therefore let us, as many as are mature, have this mind; and if in anything you think otherwise, God will reveal even this to you (Philippians 3:12-15)."

I love the two above verses. The biggest difference between me yesterday and today is that I now seek after God. The Lord loves those who seek after Him. If we seeking God then we are striving to obey the Lord. "Come near to God and He will come near to you

(James 4:8)."

Too many Christians are still trying to hold on to their old life, while seeking the new life in Christ but we must let go of the old to embrace the new. The Bible says that a man can't serve two masters.

1 Corinthians 6:12 states, "Everything is permissible for me...but not everything is beneficial." I had to let go and let God direct my steps because I was sick and tired of living the way I did. I had to let go of the trash, to get the treasure. The best thing I ever did was to surrender my life to Jesus. I came to realize that I couldn't live in willful sin and expect to live a different type of life because the Bible says, "Do not be deceived; God cannot be mocked. A man reaps what he sows (Galatians 6:7)."

I always tell people that if you are happy and content with your life, keep doing what you're doing but if you want more inner joy and peace then the new life starts with a change of heart.

Psychologists state that we will never change what we tolerate. I just became so fed up with how I lived that I decided I could not tolerate the things I formally tolerated in my life. When I started reading the Scriptures in the Bible, God spoke to my heart and explained that He couldn't tolerate my old behavior.

I came to realize that my brokenness was not a permanent state, and that God could heal me. I was healed and I now know that there is a better way. Desperation can lead to many things and in my case it led to my surrender to something greater than myself.

Here is a cheat sheet to having more joy in your life

1. Downsize your doubts.

    "Do not be anxious about anything, but in every situation, by prayer and petition, with thanksgiving, present your requests to God (Philippians 4:6)."

Many of your doubts are irrational fears that you must expose for what they are. You can do so by standing on the promises of God! Speak God's promise out loud. Doubts can trigger your stress response, putting you into fight-or-flight mode. You'll feel anxious and panicky, and your anxiety can stop you from staying focused on God. Deep breathing can help you when you feel anxious. When you stop and breathe deeply, you put yourself back into rest-and-digest mode. You allow yourself to discern what's real from what's imagined.

2. Stop trying to make everyone else happy.

"Am I now trying to win the approval of human beings, or of God? Or am I trying to please people? If I were still trying to please people, I would not be a servant of Christ (Galatians 1:10)."

Want to feel happier and more confident? Let go of your need to be a people pleaser. Take responsibility for your own inner world, and quit trying to control everyone else's.

3. Get rid of your inner critic.

Ephesians 5:29 states, "For no one has ever hated his own body, but he nourishes and tenderly cares for it, as the Messiah does the church."

Proverbs 19:8 says, "To acquire wisdom is to love oneself; people who cherish understanding will prosper."

4. Love and accept yourself because God does.

Imagine fingernails scraping a chalkboard. We all cringe. That's what happens in your brain when you criticize yourself. When you criticize, your mind develops a negative thinking pattern. You should reflect on your actions, but you shouldn't criticize yourself. Inner-harshness is a bad habit that can be changed with practice.

5. Try to notice your self-critical thoughts. When that happens, recall a positive thought from the past. Take a deep breath in, then release the breath slowly. This breath draws your attention away from the criticism.

It may seem unlikely that simply recalling positive things will change your thinking. But it will, because over time your brain will rewire itself. Self-doubt and criticism are replaced with patience and understanding.

Work on breaking your habit of criticizing. Over time, you'll cast away your doubts and cultivate a serene inner space. Isaiah 26:3 states, "You will keep in perfect peace those whose minds are steadfast, because they trust in you."

6. Meditate on the Kingdom-minded things to replace self-doubt.

"Finally, brethren, whatever things are true, whatever things are noble, whatever things are just, whatever things are pure, whatever things are lovely, whatever things are of good report, if there is any virtue and if there is anything praiseworthy—meditate on these things. Philippians 4:8

Meditation makes you happier and boosts your self-confidence. With practice, you begin to notice your mind's patterns of self-limiting thoughts, and you can let them pass without believing them. I found that practicing meditation on scripture was a powerful tool for releasing self-doubt and criticism. Additionally, you can verbalize kind thoughts about yourself out loud. For example, *"I am filled with loving-kindness. I am well, peaceful and at ease, happy and free of suffering."* You can make up what lines up with God's word to help you stay focused. Feel free to tweak this as you see fit.

7. Trust God to do His part.

Joshua 1:8 states "This Book of the Law shall not depart from your mouth, but you shall meditate on it day and night, so that you may be careful to do according to all that is written in it. For then you will make your way prosperous, and then you will have good success."

Our minds are sneaky and the devil is crafty. When you envy someone's success, your deep feeling is, "They've achieved this, but I can't." You've limited yourself and created more doubts. The inherent thought is that you don't have *enough*.

Envy keeps you stuck in a self-doubting cycle. Remember that the amount of success or happiness in this world is limitless. And you have what it takes too.

Change your jealousy to genuine joy for others, and lift your self-imposed limits. You'll feel energized and inspired—ready to channel your energy into achieving your own goals and dreams. Then take one step toward that goal. Even a tiny one.

8. **Move your body every day.**

Daily exercise keeps your mind and body healthy. The increased blood flow nourishes your body and brain. You'll feel stronger and happier from the inside out. Choose something that you love, and do it a little each day. Develop inner strength, and cast away your doubts. Start today.

9. Nurture your passions and strengths.

You'll feel alive and confident when you do what you love. When you're passionate and absorbed in your task, you can easily release your doubts.

10. Accept and love yourself.

To let go of self-doubt, you must accept all aspects of your self—including your pride and your shadows. No one is perfect. In order to let go of your doubts, you must learn to be grateful for your limitations and challenges. We all carry baggage; it's a part of being human.

Starting from a place of acceptance rather than shame will make all your efforts easier. Remember that we are all human. And we all have our messy sides.

MORE KEYS FOR THE JOY-FILLED CHRISTIAN

Don't keep yourself locked in a prison of illusionary self-doubt.

Your actions start in your mind with your thoughts. Think about what you are thinking about.

Lock your doubts away and don't let them out. You've got work to do.

Connect with those around you. It's your key to unlocking long-lasting happiness.

You have unique gifts to share with the world, and only this lifetime to do so.

Joy comes from knowing who we are in Christ

Below are 48 Bible verses to empower you and remind you of who you are in Christ

I am complete in Him Who is the Head of all principality and power (**Colossians 2:10**).

I am alive with Christ (**Ephesians 2:5**).

I am free from the law of sin and death (**Romans 8:2**).

I am far from oppression, and fear does not come near me (**Isaiah 54:14**).

I am born of God, and the evil one does not touch me (**1 John 5:18**).

I am holy and without blame before Him in love (**Ephesians 1:4**; **1 Peter 1:16**).

I have the mind of Christ (**1 Corinthians 2:16**; **Philippians 2:5**).

I have the peace of God that passes all understanding (**Philippians 4:7**).

I have the Greater One living in me; greater is He Who is in me than he who is in the world (**1 John 4:4**).

I have received the gift of righteousness and reign as a king in life by Jesus Christ (**Romans 5:17**).

I have received the spirit of wisdom and revelation in the knowledge of Jesus, the eyes of my understanding being enlightened (**Ephesians 1:17-18**).

I have received the power of the Holy Spirit to lay hands on the sick and see them recover, to cast out demons, to speak with new tongues. I have power over all the power of the enemy, and nothing shall by any means harm me (**Mark 16:17-18; Luke 10:17-19**).

I have put off the old man and have put on the new man, which is renewed in the knowledge after the image of Him Who created me (**Colossians 3:9-10**).

I have given, and it is given to me; good measure, pressed down, shaken together, and running over, men give into my bosom (**Luke 6:38**).

I have no lack for my God supplies all of my need according to His riches in glory by Christ Jesus (**Philippians 4:19**).

I can quench all the fiery darts of the wicked one with my shield of faith (**Ephesians 6:16**).

I can do all things through Christ Jesus (**Philippians 4:13**).

I show forth the praises of God Who has called me out of darkness into His marvelous light (**1 Peter 2:9**).

I am God's child for I am born again of the incorruptible seed of the Word of God, which lives and abides forever (**1 Peter 1:23**).

I am God's workmanship, created in Christ unto good works (**Ephesians 2:10**).

I am a new creature in Christ (**2 Corinthians 5:17**).

I am a spirit being alive to God (**Romans 6:11;1 Thessalonians 5:23**).

I am a believer, and the light of the Gospel shines in my mind (**2 Corinthians 4:4**).

I am a doer of the Word and blessed in my actions (**James 1:22,25**).

I am a joint-heir with Christ (**Romans 8:17**).

I am more than a conqueror through Him Who loves me (**Romans 8:37**).

I am an overcomer by the blood of the Lamb and the word of my testimony (**Revelation 12:11**).

I am a partaker of His divine nature (**2 Peter 1:3-4**).

I am an ambassador for Christ (**2 Corinthians 5:20**).

I am part of a chosen generation, a royal priesthood, a holy nation, a purchased people (**1 Peter 2:9**).

I am the righteousness of God in Jesus Christ (**2 Corinthians 5:21**).

I am the temple of the Holy Spirit; I am not my own (**1 Corinthians 6:19**).

I am the head and not the tail; I am above only and not beneath (**Deuteronomy 28:13**).

I am the light of the world (**Matthew 5:14**).

I am His elect, full of mercy, kindness, humility, and longsuffering (**Romans 8:33**; **Colossians 3:12**).

I am forgiven of all my sins and washed in the Blood (**Ephesians 1:7**).

I am delivered from the power of darkness and translated into God's kingdom (**Colossians 1:13**).

I am redeemed from the curse of sin, sickness, and poverty (**Deuteronomy 28:15-68**; **Galatians 3:13**).

I am firmly rooted, built up, established in my faith and overflowing with gratitude (**Colossians 2:7**).

I am called of God to be the voice of His praise (**Psalm 66:8**; **2 Timothy 1:9**).

I am healed by the stripes of Jesus (**Isaiah 53:5**; **1 Peter 2:24**).

I am raised up with Christ and seated in heavenly places (**Ephesians 2:6**; **Colossians 2:12**).

I am greatly loved by God (**Romans 1:7**; **Ephesians 2:4**; **Colossians 3:12**; **1 Thessalonians 1:4**).

I am strengthened with all might according to His glorious power (**Colossians 1:11**).

I am submitted to God, and the devil flees from me because I resist him in the Name of Jesus (**James 4:7**).

I press on toward the goal to win the prize to which God in Christ Jesus is calling us upward (**Philippians 3:14**).

For God has not given us a spirit of fear; but of power, love, and a sound mind (**2 Timothy 1:7**).

It is not I who live, but Christ lives in me (**Galatians 2:20**).

Back Cover

Jesus wants us to have joy and tells us in John 15:11, "These things I have spoken to you, that My joy may remain in you, and that your joy may be full." This book focuses on the joy of the Lord and how any believer can make joy a daily habit. Joy is a type of "calm happiness" and most importantly, it means "to delight in God's grace. Joy and happiness is possible through Christ Jesus. Rev. Drew calls it the "happy habit", choosing joy through purposeful living and walking in the Spirit. You will see after reading this book how the joy of Jesus Christ will become your strength and foundation in your everyday life.

This is Reverend Drew's third book. His first book is entitled "Making Jesus Lord of Your Heart, a 40 day discipleship study" and his second book is "Abundant living in God's Economy" (available on Amazon). Reverend Drew founded Faith Hope Love Ministries Harlem USA (www.faithhopelove.us) in 2015 to spread the Gospel in New York City. He is an ordained minister who strives to glorify God in all that he does. He has a B.A. and a Master's Degree. He is the son of a minister. He teaches a weekly discipleship bible study focused on Christian love and preaches the Good News of Jesus

Christ in NYC. He is available for speaking engagements/sermons and Christian life-coaching sessions.

Made in the USA
Charleston, SC
12 August 2016